CREATING SPACES FOR AN AGEING SOCIETY

CREATING SPACES FOR AN AGEING SOCIETY

The Role of Critical Social Infrastructure

BY

SOPHIE YARKER
The University of Manchester, UK

United Kingdom – North America – Japan – India
Malaysia – China

Emerald Publishing Limited
Howard House, Wagon Lane, Bingley BD16 1WA, UK

First edition 2022

Reprints and permissions service
Contact: permissions@emeraldinsight.com

British Library Cataloguing in Publication Data
A catalogue record for this book is available from the British Library

ISBN: 978-1-83982-739-6 (Print)
ISBN: 978-1-83982-738-9 (Online)
ISBN: 978-1-83982-740-2 (Epub)

Printed and bound by CPI Group (UK) Ltd, Croydon, CR0 4YY

ISOQAR certified
Management System,
awarded to Emerald
for adherence to
Environmental
standard
ISO 14001:2004.

Certificate Number 1985
ISO 14001

INVESTOR IN PEOPLE

CONTENTS

ABOUT THE AUTHOR

Sophie Yarker is based in the Manchester Institute for Collaborative Research on Ageing at The University of Manchester having previously held postitions at Aberystwyth University and Newcastle University. She has an academic background in Sociology and Human Geography with a PhD in the latter from Newcastle University. Sophie has written on the subject of local belonging and attachment, urban change and age-friendly communities and published work in both academic journals and reports for third sector organisations. From 2021 she has been working on the 'Population ageing and urbanisation' project funded by the Leverhulme Trust which is an interdisciplinary and cross-national comparative research project into ageing in place in cities. Sophie is also Deputy Director of the Manchester Urban Ageing Research Group.

ACKNOWLEDGEMENTS

This book would not have been possible without the insights, collaboration and support of a number of people and organisations. The ideas informing my work on social infrastructure emerged from my time as Research Fellow on the Ambition for Ageing Programme. I would therefore like to thank the programme staff based at the Greater Manchester Centre for Voluntary Organisation, in particular John Hannen, Kirsty Bagnall and Sarah Wilkinson, for their contributions towards the ideas within this text and for their continued interest in the work. This book has also benefited from funding from The National Lottery Community Fund and the Leverhulme Trust and support from the Greater Manchester Ageing Hub and the Manchester Institute for Collaborative Research on Ageing.

I am hugely grateful to have found and become involved with the Manchester Urban Ageing Research Group whose research interests and expertise have inspired and helped develop my interest in social infrastructure and age-friendly communities. I would like to give special thanks to Chris Phillipson and Tine Buffel for their continued support, invaluable academic guidance and the opportunity to write this book in the first place.

I would like to acknowledge the anonymous reviewers of both the book proposal and earlier drafts of the manuscript for their supportive and helpful comments which have no doubt improved the end result. I would also like to thank the team at Emerald Publishing for their patience and advice needed to bring the book to fruition.

Finally, the majority of this book was written in 2020 during several national lockdowns in response to the coronavirus pandemic. My experience of those lockdowns would have been very different had it not been for the many socially distanced brews and laughter I shared with the women who lived in my building; the women who have now become some of my dearest friends. Therefore, I would like to thank Ruth Cousins, Chanel Goy and Emily Sayle for their unfailing support and friendship during this time.

1

THINKING INFRASTRUCTURALLY ABOUT
AN AGEING SOCIETY

Upon hearing the word 'infrastructure' your mind might immediately go to the hard and physical infrastructures of roads, dams, communication networks and power plants, the type of infrastructures often referred to as 'critical' signifying their central role in keeping the economy going. This book is concerned with a particular type of infrastructure, social infrastructure, the places and organisations that keep the *social* economy going by allowing us to have social interactions, develop social connections and maintain relationships. Eric Klinenberg (2018, p. 17) defines social infrastructure expansively as;

> *Public institutions, such as libraries, schools, playgrounds, parks, athletic fields, and swimming pools…sidewalks, courtyards, community gardens, and other spaces that invite people into the public realm. Community organisations, including churches and civic associations, act as social infrastructures when they have an established physical space where people can assemble, as do regularly scheduled markets for food, furniture, clothing, art and other consumer goods. Commercial establishments can also be important parts of the social infrastructure.*

Much like its physical counterpart, social infrastructure is largely taken for granted by the majority of the population. Infrastructure is in the background, keeping things going and going mostly unnoticed. That is, until it fails. Ask yourself how often do you notice and comment upon a well-surfaced and maintained road compared to how often you notice and comment on one riddled with potholes? Or how often do you spend time thinking about the privilege of having electricity in your house? The answer is you probably don't until there is a power failure. When infrastructure fails or becomes absent altogether is when we notice it the most and when it can, all of a sudden, become a pressing concern.

The coronavirus pandemic that began in 2020, and the social distancing measures brought into place as a result, forced us all to reflect upon the spaces in which we have our social interactions in a way we had perhaps not considered before. As well as no longer being able to meet with friends and family in public places, many of us also found ourselves cut off from the multiple smaller, more fleeting and seemingly more inconsequential interactions we have on a daily basis. We no longer saw the same familiar faces at the bus stop on our commute to the office, for example, nor were we able to exchange a few words with those we see at the gym. Instead, for many of us the sphere of face-to-face social interactions contracted to include a limited set of interactions perhaps with our immediate neighbours, with those we might come to recognise over time in the local park or with the staff in shops nearest to us. The majority of research discussed in this book on how we use public space was published before 2020; however, this research still has important lessons for how we might think about social infrastructure differently as we start to recover economically and socially from the pandemic. The unprecedented measures taken to limit social contact in our everyday lives has caused us all to pause and think about what social interactions do we value the most and what are the important spaces in our communities that facilitate these interactions.

However, the undervaluing of our social infrastructure runs deep. Thinking in terms of 'physical' and 'social' infrastructure might itself be unhelpful if we are trying to increase the profile and significance of social infrastructure. Dividing the two can serve to reproduce a false division between the relative importance of different types of infrastructures with the 'hard' physical infrastructures of roads and power plants being seen as vital to the economy and social infrastructures such as libraries and parks thought of as nice to have but not essential.

The relative value of social and hard infrastructures is also complicated by the fact that it can be more difficult to identify, measure and quantify social impacts. The impacts of a new high speed rail link, for example, can be measured in passenger numbers or the number of new businesses relocations. Measuring the number of social interactions and the value of the networks they might go on to produce is more elusive. The more subjective nature of social benefits, either to the individual user or to the wider community, means that they can be more difficult and problematic to measure.

These issues of subjectivity versus objectivity and the respective credibility that can be associated are mirrored in discussions around the natural and social sciences. The labelling of the former as the 'hard' sciences has brought with it the assumption that natural sciences are more complex and specialist, whilst social sciences are easier to comprehend. Duncan Watts at Microsoft Research in New York City has pointed out: 'Everyone has experience of being human, and so the vast majority of findings in social science coincide with something that we have either experienced or can imagine experiencing' (quoted in *Nature* editorial, 2012). However instead of this being seen as a virtue, it can often serve to undermine the value of social science research. We see similar accusations levelled at the qualitative methodologies that are more commonly associated with the social sciences with questions being raised around their reliability, rigour and susceptibility to bias. In short, the social sciences and the qualitative methodologies have a history of being viewed as more inconsequential than natural sciences. We see a similarly unhelpful division when we talk about skills in the workplace. Social skills such as being a good listener or being able to develop positive working relationships are often referred to as 'soft' skills which seems to position them as somehow lesser in importance than Information Technology (IT) or presentation skills, for example. It seems that to use 'social' as an adjective is to undermine something's relative worth and importance. This book argues that the social is critical and that social infrastructure is also critical infrastructure.

THE INFRASTRUCTURAL TURN

This book both draws upon and hopes to contribute to what has been referred to as an infrastructural turn within the social sciences. This is a turn towards an explicit focus on infrastructure as a way of studying and understanding the social world. It has resulted in a new wave of interdisciplinary, and increasingly qualitative, thinking on how the functions and impacts of infrastructures shape countries, regions, cities and neighbourhoods.

Latham & Layton argue that to study social infrastructures is to study 'one way that the good city might be realised' (2019, p. 10). By thinking infrastructurally, they continue, social scientists are better placed to 'consider the kinds and qualities of facilities that allow social life to happen, the kind of sociality that is afforded by them, and how this can be recognised as a public life' (Latham & Layton, 2019, p. 4). For the purposes of this book, thinking infrastructurally allows us to think about the kinds of sociality needed as we age and what facilities and qualities of public spaces can provide opportunities for social connections for older people.

Whilst social infrastructures are important for everyone, Klinenberg argues they are especially important for children, older people and for those whose limited mobility or lack of autonomy binds them more closely to the places where they live. This is especially true for older people living in more economically deprived neighbourhoods (Hickman, 2013). But why are these spaces so important? Klinenberg (2018) stresses social infrastructure is necessary for nurturing public life but also for addressing and preventing some of the most pressing concerns of contemporary urban life; countering social isolation, negotiating difference and creating places for all;

> *When social infrastructure is robust, it fosters contact, mutual support, and collaboration among friends and neighbours; when it is degraded, it inhibits social activity, leaving families and individuals to fend for themselves.*
>
> *(Klinenberg, 2018, p. 5)*

This was demonstrated most clearly in Klinenberg's analysis of the differences in neighbourhood death rates during the 1995 Chicago heat wave (2015). Studying two low-income neighbourhoods, Klinenberg argued that the significantly lower death rates of one of those neighbourhoods could be attributed to the presence of diverse, good quality and accessible social infrastructure. Conversely, the neighbourhood with higher heat-attributed deaths had very little accessible public space nor amenities. Klinenberg concluded that when community members have more opportunities to bump into one another, exchange pleasantries and become, to some degree, familiar with each other, they are more likely to check on neighbours during a crisis, offer help and assistance and to receive help if it was offered. For Klinenberg, in this case the sociality supported by social infrastructure saved lives.

Several reports have come to similar conclusions in the context of the COVID-19 pandemic. A report measuring the changing nature of community in the United Kingdom looked at both physical assets and civic institutions, as well as less tangible dimensions such as social relationships and positive social norms in communities in the United Kingdom and found that local authority areas with the lowest COVID-19 related death rates also tended to have higher numbers of community-owned assets, more residents who were members of and actively involved in groups and organisations and higher levels of volunteering (Tanner, O'Shaughnessy, Krasniqi, & Blagden, 2020). Better social infrastructure may have translated into more locally based support. A report for the Bennett Institute for Public Policy (2021) analysed data from Covid-19 Mutual Aid UK and concluded that places with more community facilities had higher levels of mutual aid activity during the pandemic. Although the authors of this report caution against taking this as evidence of a direct causational relationship (and that factors such as educational levels and household incomes would need to be taken into consideration too, for example) they do conclude that 'communities with better social infrastructure find it easier to respond to, withstand and recover from crisis' (Kelsey & Kenny, 2021, p. 6).

Further research will be needed into how different communities responded to the pandemic, but we can perhaps begin to build a hypothesis that communities with more amenities, parks and public libraries, etc. were better equipped to respond to the crisis because this social infrastructure had facilitated social connections and networks between residents that was able to respond swiftly and provide vital support locally. In the context of ageing populations, fractured societies and alienated communities, an understanding of how we can use the structures in our neighbourhoods to create social connections seems a pressing one. In the context of a global pandemic, it gains even more urgency. Social infrastructure therefore takes on its own a critical role.

Taking an infrastructural approach also provides a way of understanding the elusive concept of community. As a concept, community has a lively albeit complex history. Many texts before this one have attempted to define it and chronical its development (see Crow, 2018) and the intention is not to replicate any of those discussions here, instead, as part of the introduction to the concept of social infrastructure this chapter will briefly consider how it can be used to study and understand community.

Community can be very loosely defined as a group of people who share something in common. This commonality can be associated with a particular geographical location, shared identity or shared interests. Belonging to or identifying with a community infers some degree of connectedness that Crow describes as 'underpinning the social solidarity of community members' (2018, p. 3). This solidary can form the basis of community-building practices such as co-operation, mutual aid and reciprocity. How to operationalise social solidarity and connectedness has been a recurring question for community studies. Social capital, social networks and social cohesion are just some of the conceptual avenues that have been explored. If social connections are the starting point for the formation of community then examining the spaces and places, where social connections are formed, allows us to shed light on the beginnings of community.

The story of social infrastructure is also the story of community. Both the state of our social infrastructure and how we use and experience it can tell us a lot about the places in which we go about our everyday lives. A narrative of decline has come to dominate discussions around community in contemporary Western societies demonstrated by a UK poll in 2020 which found 71% of respondents felt there had been a decline in community during their lifetime (Tanner et al., 2020). Social infrastructure, either directly or indirectly, has become part of this narrative of decline often expressed through pointing to a deterioration in social infrastructure. There is some tangible evidence for this. In the United Kingdom, 26% of pubs have closed since 2001, 28% of libraries have closed or reduced their services since 2005, and post offices have reduced from just over 22,000 in 1982 to just over 11,000 by 2018 (Tanner et al., 2020). People point to the decline of social infrastructure as evidence of both physical deterioration but also often as a manifestation of a feeling of coming apart from the places where they live themselves, of feeling rootless or culturally displaced. This is often felt more deeply for older residents who may have lived in a place for longer periods of time and hold longer memories of a place. There is also worrying evidence about the long-term changes affecting communities. The Office of National Statistics (ONS) review of trends in social capital in the United Kingdom highlighted significant developments over the past decade, with evidence of less positive engagement with neighbours, less help being given to groups such as older people and a reduced sense of belonging to the communities in which we live (cited in Phillipson et al., 2020).

However, it is important to remember there was never a golden era of community. Most of us use the term 'the good old days' with a sense of irony and an awareness that, in many ways, we are a lot better off than previous generations. However, as is argued by a UK report on the Politics of Belonging, 'quality of life has been deteriorating – in the strength of community and sense of neighbourliness that defines (their) place – and this loss matters deeply to people's sense of belonging' (Onward, 2020, p. 3). To dismiss a feeling of being adrift from a place as simply a nostalgia for another period in history is to misunderstand these sentiments. As Carol Stack (1996) argues, no one is seeking to turn back the clock. People are seeking a place in which their lives and their strivings matter and will make a difference. In order for a place to offer such opportunities, it must be equipped with the social infrastructure necessary to support social interactions and the development of social networks between residents. So, the loss of social infrastructure is not simply about the lack of amenities, but it is about the loss of having something in our neighbourhoods to belong to. Social infrastructure is the scaffolding that enables us to build and be part of a sense of community where we live.

AGEING POPULATIONS

This book considers the role of social infrastructures in the context of an ageing population. Population ageing is one of the defining characteristics of the twentieth century and is set to continue. There has been an unprecedented increase in the average life expectancy as well as a rapid fall in fertility rates in many countries across the world. In the Global North, the percentage of the population aged 60 years and older has grown from 12% in 1950 to 23% in 2013 and is expected to rise to 32% in 2050. In the Global South, we find the same pattern but occurring at a slower rate with the percentage of over 60s growing from 6% in 1950 to 9% in 2013; however, this is expected to accelerate to 19% by 2050 (Buffel & Phillipson, 2018).

The result of these trends has been a huge expansion in both policy and research interest in ageing populations. This has focused on a range of questions from those of physical and mental health, to financial security, civic participation and employment. The particular area of ageing this book is interested in is that of social connections and how these can be developed and maintained in later life to support healthy ageing in its broadest sense. This is part of a broader recognition within ageing policy and research that is it not simply enough to be able to live a long life, or even a long life free from life-limiting illness or disability (although we might all hope for that), but that we must aspire to more than this. We must strive for an experience of later life where we feel connected and valued, visible and useful much of which stems from our social relationships with others. Humans are social beings, and social connections are important for all age groups, but there is a growing recognition of the particular importance for our wellbeing of social connections in later life.

Addressing Loneliness and Isolation – The Importance of Social Connections in Later Life

The shift in focus in how we consider the challenges of an ageing population means that wellbeing questions of how our social connections and our relationships can support us as we age have become vital ones for us to understand. Thus, loneliness (and the associated concept of social isolation) has moved significantly up the ageing agenda. Whilst it is difficult to know with any degree of certainty what the prevalance of loneliness amongst the older population is at any given time, research from the UK-based charity Age UK argues that we are facing a crisis within the older population of limited and decreasing social contact with others. Their research suggests that half a million older people living in the United Kingdom go at least five or six days without seeing or speaking to anyone and that two-fifths of older people say the television is their main source of company (Bolton, 2012).

The terms loneliness and social isolation tend to be used interchangeably, but they are quite distinct concepts and require separate attention. Social isolation is the objective absence of social contacts whereas loneliness is a subjective negative experience that results from inadequate meaningful connections and where there exists a discrepancy between one's social and emotional needs and our actual experience. The phrase 'lonely in a crowd' is a useful one here in thinking about the distinction. Someone can have a busy work life that brings them into contact with many different colleagues. They can have an active social life with multiple social engagements. They may even have people they call 'friends' but if they feel they have no one to talk to about personal or emotional matters, or if they feel none of the people around them really understand them, they might still experience the feeling of being lonely. Those who have a partner or spouse may be shielded from loneliness to some extent, but this is not a given. The relationship may not meet the person's emotional needs, and there is evidence to suggest that single people have larger social networks than those who are part of a couple (Klinenberg, 2013). This also raises the distinction between emotional loneliness and social loneliness, the former being a feeling of having no one close to talk to and confide in and the latter a feeling of no one to socialise with. Equally, a person can be socially isolated and have very limited social contact with others, but they might not feel lonely if they are satisfied with this arrangement and if it is through choice.

Nonetheless, the majority of us need at least some form of social contact with others, even if this is fleeting and irregular. Loneliness and social isolation are not just concerning for the individual; they are public health issues. There is a wealth of research indicating the health and wellbeing benefits of social connections and the consequences of being without them. For example, social connections can act as a buffer to negative life events, giving us both the tangible and emotional resources to be able to cope with life's adversities and adapt to new challenges. Having social connections can also promote engagement in social and civic life such as having a friend to introduce you to volunteering at a local organisation or having someone to attend a sports club with, for example. Being lonely can also have physiological impacts. It can affect a person's sleep, increase their risk of hypertension, lower the immune system and leave them more susceptible to depression (Bolton, 2012). At its most stark, the impacts of loneliness and social isolation can be seen in their effects on mortality. A meta-analysis of 148 studies into social relationships and mortality found that there was a 50% increase in the likelihood of survival for those with strong social connections. This was regardless of initial health conditions. The same study also concluded that loneliness was more harmful than not exercising, twice as harmful as obesity and the equivalent, in terms of stress on the body, of smoking 15 cigarettes a day or of being an alcoholic (Holt-Lunstad, Smith, & Layton, 2010). Social connections are therefore not just a matter of having a social life, they are about having a good quality of life and, in some instances, they are a matter of life and death itself. Therefore, the focus on loneliness and social isolation in ageing research has contributed to the consideration of *quality* of life as we age, i.e. thinking of ageing not just in a physiological sense of the absence of illness or mobility issues but in terms of overall life satisfaction.

The extent of loneliness within the older population is difficult to assess. How loneliness is measured in population level surveys differs between studies, meaning it is very difficult to compare levels of loneliness in any given population over time or between different groups. Equally, loneliness is a not a static state. Loneliness can be transitory or persistent (Scharf, 2011). People can experience periods of loneliness for a time, often associated with a loss or change in circumstances, but this can be overcome. However, for some people loneliness can be more of a permanent state due to problematic relationships or their own personal circumstances. Loneliness has been found to be particularly temporal for older people, with certain seasons, days of the week and even times of day having an impact on whether a person reports feeling lonely or not.

So, what are the risk factors associated with social isolation and loneliness and how might growing older affect this? Victor and Pikhartova (2020) identify four categories of risk associated with loneliness in later life. Firstly, there can be interpersonal situations such as the strength and quality of relationships people have with friends, family or neighbours. Secondly, life stage events, sometimes referred to as transitions, such as retirement, loss or health issues may cause a person to lose social connections. Thirdly, wider social structures such as poverty, health inequalities and discrimination can impact on a person's access to social networks and their ability to make social connections, and finally, the social environment in which a person lives will play a determining role in the opportunities people have for making social connections and developing relationships. This refers to things such as the different hobbies or activities a person is involved with, the level of neighbour interaction as well as spaces and facilities for social interaction in their neighbourhood. In other words, the social infrastructures available to a person.

How loneliness and isolation are experienced by different groups of older people is also largely unknown. In particular, we know very little about the experiences of older adults from different minority ethnic groups (Lewis & Cotterell, 2017). Some research suggests that rates of loneliness might be higher for older people from some minority ethnic groups compared to the wider population. Victor, Burholt, and Martin (2012), for example, studied loneliness in older people living in the United Kingdom who were originally from China, Africa, the Caribbean, Pakistan and Bangladesh and found varying rates of reported loneliness from 24% of participants to up to 50% compared with rates of loneliness for older White British adults that were around 8–10%. There is a lack of research evidence as to why some minority ethnic groups might experience higher levels of loneliness, but the wider literature on risk factors gives us some clues. For example, we know that older people living on low incomes and in more deprived neighbourhoods are at a higher risk of social isolation, so the higher numbers of older people from some minority ethnic communities, especially the Black community and some sections of the South Asian communities living in low income areas would suggest these individuals might be more socially isolated (Jivraj & Khan, 2013; cited in Lewis & Cotterell, 2017). Also, we know that having poor health or limited mobility can increase social isolation and that older people from minority ethnic groups are more likely to experience health inequalities; so, once again, this might increase the prevalence of social isolation amongst these groups. However, this causation has not been proven. In addition, experiences of racism and discrimination over the lifecourse can exacerbate inequalities, leaving communities marginalised and individuals at greater risk of social isolation (Burholt, Dobbs, & Victor, 2016) although the link between racism and ageism is even less understood and requires further research (Phillipson, 2015).

A study by Victor et al. found that older Indian adults living in the United Kingdom reported similar or lower levels of loneliness compared with the White British population. From what we know about the importance of social contact through family and the wider community, it is reasonable to suggest that members of some minority ethnic groups may have some protection from social isolation due to being part of a faith-based network or by being part of a larger extended family. However, we have already seen that being surrounded by people does not necessarily mean people are not lonely. In addition, there is evidence to suggest that commonly held beliefs around the prevalence of multi-generational households and extended family networks in some minority ethnic communities (in particular communities of South Asian heritage) might not provide the level of protection from social isolation as once thought

(Phillipson, 2015). In short, we do not know nearly enough about how social isolation and loneliness in later life affects different groups, and therefore much more research is needed into its prevalence, risk factors and therefore potential ways of addressing it that meet the needs of an increasingly diverse older population.

This book focuses its attention on how the environment in which a person lives impacts on their access to social relationships by considering how the social infrastructures of our neighbourhoods provide opportunities for social connections. Such a focus aligns with suggestions in the literature that there tends to be an over-emphasis on individual level risk factors within the existing research into loneliness in later life (Victor & Pikhartova, 2020) and a call for a consideration of a broader range of macro- and meso-level factors that might contribute to loneliness in later life. The meso-level includes attending to the social infrastructure in a person's environment and considering how this might help or hinder the development of social connections.

The interventions of human geographers, along with environmental gerontology, have established the importance of place and the environment in which we age. Victor and Pikhartiva, for example, found that the quality of the locality in which people live (as measured in their study by deprivation) had an independent effect on loneliness in later life. The differences in urban and rural environments have also been considered although with mixed results. Although cities might provide high density living with greater access to services and amenities for older people, there are many challenges associated with urban living that can impede the lives of older people. Equally, although rural communities can potentially offer greater inclusivity and a sense of community, rural places can be physically isolated from services and amenities as well as experiencing their own levels of deprivation (Heley & Jones, 2013). In short, there is limited and inconsistent empirical evidence on the effects of different environments, and many of these studies stop short of considering the finer detail of what precise features of a neighbourhood support social connections for older people. The review of literatures presented in this book start to fill in some of these details by looking at what types of social infrastructure support different types of social connections for older people.

A focus on social isolation and loneliness have been incredibly important in shifting discussions on ageing from an emphasis on frailty, falls and dementia towards a more holistic understanding of health that encompasses quality of life and wellbeing. A recognition of the role that place and neighbourhood play in shaping our experience of ageing has translated into a growing literature on ageing in place and age-friendly communities, both emphasising the importance of neighbourhood, and where people live, as vital for quality of life as we age. This is not just about being able to have social interactions with people but is also about older people being included, respected, valued, seen and engaged, as well as connected.

Age-Friendly Cities and Communities

In recognition of the importance of the environment in which we age various frameworks and initiatives have emerged aiming to promote and implement environmental factors that can support ageing. These initiatives come under different names such as 'liveable places', 'life-time neighbourhoods', 'the village movement', 'elder-friendly' and the one which will be used most often in this book, 'age-friendly'. This reflects the terminology of the World Health Organisation (WHO) who have produced guidance to identify the key characteristics of an age-friendly environment and to help countries meet the WHO policy goal of supporting older people to remain in their chosen homes and communities for as long as is possible and appropriate. An age-friendly environment can be defined as a place where older people are actively involved, valued and supported with infrastructure and services that affectively accommodate their needs (Alley, Liebig, Pynoos, Banerjee, & Choi, 2007, p. 4).

In 2007, the WHO launched the Global Network of Age Friendly Cities (GNAFC) in an attempt to encourage cities and communities to implement age-friendly policy recommendations. The addition of 'Communities' was added in 2010. In 2020, the number of cities belonging to the network stood at just over 1,000 representing the commitment of 41 countries across the world. Reflecting the different dimensions of age-friendly environments, there are different approaches that can be taken in implementing age-friendly work. Lui, Everingham, Warburton, Cuthill, and Bartlett (2009) have produced a helpful typology to categorise these approaches which include different dimensions such as the built environment, service provision and opportunities for social and civic participation as well different approaches such as top-down and bottom-up governance. The WHO emphasises that belonging to the network is a demonstration of *commitment* to age-friendly principles rather than the achievement of some objective standard in itself. Age-friendly environments are context specific, requiring a mix of different approaches in different places; however, Scharlach (2016) stresses the importance of attending to *both* the physical and social infrastructure in building age-friendly cities and communities, an argument of the centre of this book.

WHAT THIS BOOK WILL DO

Existing research tells us that community matters for older people and the experience of ageing. Existing research also tells us that shared spaces matter at a community level for cohesion and engagement. Therefore, this book agues firstly, that we need to better understand what types of social connections are beneficial to ageing, and secondly, we need a greater understanding of how and where these connections are built, maintained and supported through shared spaces.

In the next chapter, the theoretical underpinnings of an infrastructural approach to age-friendly communities will be sketched out. This includes a discussion of how we can understand the uses of different types of social connections through the concept of social capital and how these connections might be made through the different types of interaction we have. This involves looking at other areas of research on interactions in public spaces to see what we might learn from thinking about interactions that might support age-friendly principles.

The discussion in Chapters 3–5 present reviews of literature and existing research on different types of social infrastructures categorised by this book as outdoor venues and public space, group activities, public services and institutions and commercial venues. The research reviewed for these chapters is international and interdisciplinary. Relevant areas of literature have been identified in human geography, sociology and urban studies as well as social and environmental gerontology and beyond. The majority of research presented in these chapters is based on findings from high-income countries in the Global North, and therefore the conclusions drawn will only have relevance in this context. It is most certainly a short-coming of this book that a consideration of age-friendly environments in less developed economies and in the context of the Global South is not made. However, the contexts of ageing populations are too diverse to be given proper consideration within this one text, so the decision has been made to focus where there was the most research evidence already in existence to allow for a more detailed discussion to be had.

In each category of social infrastructure, two or three examples of particular spaces have been selected to illustrate the discussion. The literature reviews presented in these chapters are far from exhaustive. Instead, they are intended to give the reader an indication of how these spaces might function as social infrastructure and their relevance to older populations. Chapters 3–5 reflect a hybrid of what Arksey and O'Malley (2005) define as a systematic review and a scoping review of the literature. That is to say that the book will map relevant literature by identifying which scholarly fields have engaged with the fields of social infrastructure and shared neighbourhood spaces, but it will also look in more detail at the relevant findings of this work and tease out what this might mean for ageing.

The research questions guiding the selection of literature have been 'how do different types of social infrastructure support older people? What social interactions and connections are being developed in these spaces? and what might the impacts of this be on the wider community?' This reflects the fact that many of the studies drawn upon will not be explicitly focused on the older population, and therefore the analysis of the book asks what we can learn from these studies that might be applicable or relevant when considering how older people experience neighbourhoods. For the purpose of this book, 'older people' will be defined as those aged 50 and above with recognition that there will be significant divergence of experience within that cohort.

Chapter 6 turns briefly to the questions of intergenerational connections and encounters. Drawing on some of the research presented in the book, it looks at what we already know about social relationships outside the family between those of different ages and asks how we might better understand and support these connections. Chapter 7 looks at the external pressures acting on our social infrastructures and considers how processes of urban development and austerity can erode our social infrastructure and the impact this might have on age-friendly work. The chapter ends by turning to the Coronavirus pandemic to think about what impacts this is already having on the social fabric of our society and what this might continue to look like in the future.

In the final concluding chapter, the main points from the book are reiterated before outlining a new research agenda for an infrastructural approach to age-friendly communities. This takes what we have discovered as important through this book and asks how we can further investigate and understand how older people use social infrastructures and how this can support age-friendly work. In doing so, the concluding chapter recognises this book as very much a starting point for future research. It is hoped that by at least bringing together in one place the diverse literatures on ageing, community and social interactions, presenting a synthesis of some of those literatures, and in identifying some of the gaps, that this book can be used as a basis for further research and policy conversations.

2

UNDERSTANDING SOCIAL INFRASTRUCTURE AND SOCIAL CONNECTIONS

This chapter will introduce some of the key concepts that underpin this book. In the previous chapter, social infrastructure was introduced as the spaces in our communities that create opportunities for people to have social interactions and to build social connections. This chapter will unpack this in more detail looking at what spaces and places we are concerned with and what types of interactions are important. The chapter will also explore several related concepts needed to support a theoretical framework of social infrastructure and will conclude by outlining what such a framework has to offer the study of age-friendly communities.

A CONCEPTUAL FRAMEWORK OF SOCIAL INFRASTRUCTURE

Klinenberg (2018) describes social infrastructure as the background technological networks that support urban life and allow social, economic, cultural and political life to happen. These infrastructures underpin society. As outlined in the introduction, this book follows Klinenberg's expansive interpretation of social infrastructure that includes community spaces such as community hubs, public services such as libraries and schools, public spaces such as parks and squares, as well as commercial spaces such as shops, markets, cafes, banks and post offices. This book follows the approach of Klinenberg in defining social infrastructure as physical spaces of connection. Some definitions also include social networks and relationships however the approach of this book will be to separate the tangible from the intangible so that we can better understand the types of connection different physical spaces facilitate.

This expansive definition is useful in a number of ways, not least because it allows us to remain open to the diversity of spaces that different groups of people might view as important for their social lives. Different people use different social spaces. For example, some people would not consider a betting shop as a key part of their social infrastructure. This might not be a space they visit at all, yet for others, it might be the only public space where they have social interactions with others on any given day. Likewise, for those who use them regularly, gyms and leisure centres provide the setting for a core part of their social interactions, whereas for others it might be religious spaces that fulfil this need. Therefore, if we are to remain alert to the importance of social connections for older people in particular, we need to work with an understanding of social infrastructure that can incorporate the diversity of social needs and habits within the older population.

The Places

The types of spaces this book is interested in have often been conceptualised as third places drawing on Ray Oldenburg's influential book *The Great Good Places* (1989). This defines third places as being any space that has the capacity to facilitate social interaction and therefore has the potential for the building of social capital. It distinguishes third places as being outside of the home (the first place), as well as outside our place of employment (the second place). For Oldenburg and Bissett (1982), the value of third places comes from the opportunities they give people to come into contact with those who have different backgrounds and experiences to themselves. They argued that living in a community provided people with opportunities for social relationships and experiences with a diversity of human beings; 'these social arenas historically provided people with a larger measure of their sense of wholeness and distinctiveness' (Oldenburg & Bissett, 1982, p. 267). By coming into contact with difference, third places allow us to have a sense of ourselves in relation to others. Third places are not just important for social connections but of our own sense of connection to the world, or place within it and for understanding and learning how we relate to others. Both the individual and community-level benefits of third places will be explored in greater detail throughout this book.

Oldenburg and Bissett offer several characteristics of a third place. Firstly, they should be on neutral ground and somewhere accessible during the course of a person's everyday life. This does not mean they have to be visited daily, but that there is the option to do so. It also means somewhere that is ordinary and within the scope of a person's daily life. A traditional market would be an example to fit this description. Linked to the idea of neutrality is Oldenburg's assertion that third places can act as a leveller and encourage use from people of all backgrounds.

Third places should also have no obvious host according to Oldenburg and Bissett. They should be open and accessible to all but with no one group or individual acting as the owners of that space. A third place should be used by different groups of people each feeling their own sense of ownership for the time they use it but also sharing with others. An example might be a public library which hosts parent and toddler groups as well as skills sessions for jobseekers. These different groups share the space and co-exist alongside each other, but the library is not 'owned' by either. Another example would be public parks and green spaces; they are open to all for a diversity of different purposes; dog walking, playing and exercise at any time during the parks' opening hours.

The importance of physical characteristics of third places is also worth noting. Oldenburg asserts that they should be local in the sense that they are walkable and accessible. They need to be physically located in their neighbourhoods and they need to be accessible on foot in order to facilitate the casual drop-by nature of the interaction that having to drive or take public transport to a venue might undermine. In order to create an atmosphere that is welcoming and open, Oldenburg states that third places should, for the most part, be unassuming and unremarkable in their appearance, and they should be accessible at extended times of the day so that they are available to members of the community with different schedules and different paid and unpaid working responsibilities.

The characteristics of third places offered by Oldenburg and Bissett give us a useful starting point from which to identify social infrastructure and think about how it might be relevant to older people. However, there are some aspects of these characteristics that need further discussion and, in some cases, may need to be re-thought. The first is the idea that third places should not have an obvious host. Whilst it may be true that spaces used by a diversity of groups with no one 'owner' might facilitate the ability to mix with others, the research presented in this book, especially around community and voluntary organisations, stresses the importance of someone who can bring people into a space and make them welcome. This does not always have to be a formal role, but the importance of people in a space to help create the right conditions for others to feel welcome is essential. For example, Stewart, Browning, and Sims (2015) found that shop assistants played an important role in cultivating the right conditions for social interaction in their store, often taking the lead themselves in making social connections with and between customers.

The second point on which this book challenges the traditional understanding of third places is their need to be local. Whilst this might be desirable, research discussed in this book has found that if a place is important to the social and cultural identity of a person, then they are often willing to travel outside of their local area to visit it. Therefore, a more useful discussion in age-friendly debates might be how to facilitate access to important social infrastructures for all groups of older people, through public or community transport for example. Finally, this book will also consider in greater depth some of the power relations at work either within third places or acting on them which can reproduce the social exclusion of older people belonging to marginalised groups. Urban change and processes of gentrification, for example, can lead to a proliferation of new commercial establishments that *could* act as third places such as new cafes; however, these are not always inclusive, especially not to older people, and this can lead to older people feeling culturally and social excluded from some commercial spaces (Buffel & Phillipson, 2019).

Finally, a caveat needs to be included in this discussion regarding the distinction Oldenburg draws between third place and the workplace and home. Over a certain age, most people will retire and no longer be visiting a place of work, assuming of course they have a paid occupation to retire from. Therefore, the consideration of social interactions occurring in a workplace (the second place) may no longer be relevant here. However, this is not to say that social networks developed through a person's working life may not continue to provide an important source of social connection and support, but this does tend to assume some sort of stability and careers trajectory within a person's working life that may not be applicable to those who have never been in paid employment or for those who had more sporadic and less stable periods of employment. Oldenburg's presumption of certain, middle class, professional experiences and gendered positions is also used by many feminist writers to critique his assumption of the home as a space offering a safe haven and positive, supportive relationships. For many, this is not the case.

The Interactions

If social infrastructure is about understanding where social interaction takes place, we need to understand what exactly we are looking for when we say 'interaction'. Does this mean people coming together to have meaningful discussions around a common purpose, for example? Does it mean people having a one-off encounter or building friendships or does it mean non-verbal interaction and simply recognising the same faces over time? Social interaction can mean all of these things, and all are relevant for a discussion of the types of social connections that support older people.

For Oldenburg and Bissett, conversation is the main activity in third places, even though the setting might actually be a place for sports, eating or shopping, it must also allow for conversation to occur. They draw on Georg Simmel's concept of pure sociability (1949) to explain the types of social interactions that might be important for this. For Simmel, sociability is found in all forms of interaction with others; however, he made the distinction that the type of sociability needed is *pure* sociability. These are not the types of social interactions involved in the outward status we may perform at work, for example, or, in what Simmel refers to, as purposive forms of association where we are engaging in social interaction with a particular purpose in mind and under the guise of a particular part of our identity. For example, whilst at work we may engage in a certain style of sociality in order to perform our work identities. Some topics of conversation might be considered more appropriate than others, and our patterns of speech and vocabulary may be more formal. Pure sociability, on the other hand, is the casual engagements, small talk and light-touch interactions where a person can 'express their unique sense of individuality'. This type of sociability is less concerned with conveying our status or identity and more about connecting with the other person, even if this is only in a small way. It is this type of sociability that Simmel argued was so important to supporting social life.

Although conversation certainly forms the basis of many social connections, research into the importance of social connections in later life suggests that this might not necessarily always be the case. Hickman (2013) argued that for people who are the most isolated, seeing familiar faces or even seeing people at all was a vital form of social interaction. As a result, Hickman expanded the definition of 'interaction' to include non-verbal interactions in his study of neighbourhood infrastructure in six deprived neighbourhoods in the United Kingdom. Drawing on work from British community studies in the 1960s and 1970s, he argued that Hunter and Suttles (1972) concept of the 'face-block' is still relevant especially in lower income communities and for other social groups that tend to spend more time in their neighbourhoods, such as older people. The concept of a face-block community was one in which people are aware of each other and where there is some level of recognition, but they do not necessarily know each other's identities and do not formally interact with each other. These are the people who you might see regularly in your local grocery store or at the bus stop. You assume they live in the same neighbourhood as you but you do not *know* them. This level of familiarity in a community can be incredibly important for those who are socially isolated. Research has also found that these types of non-verbal interactions can have just as much impact in making older people feel connected to and visible in their local neighbourhoods. Sometimes, just being able to see social life, from the living room window, for example, can help a person feel more connected to some form of sociability in their communities (Gardner, 2011).

These types of non-verbal and fleeting engagements can also have benefits for the wider community. 'Low-level' sociability, such as opening doors for people and saying hello in the street, represents an important facet of mutual acknowledgement (Laurier & Philo, 2006; Thrift, 2005) and, although small, can become meaningful when repeated over time. This is because they have the potential to express shared feelings such as happiness, fear, frustration and hope that can hold potential for more profound social relations (Askins, 2016). Amin (2002) argues that these 'micro-publics' are often more authentic and therefore meaningful when they are allowed to occur organically through everyday social encounter rather than at larger scale engineered events. Over time these small, often fleeting, interactions can develop an 'ethics of togetherness' (Jacobs, 1992; Sennett, 2017) or social surplus (Amin, 2002) from which a shared sense of trust and tolerance is grown. 'The sum of such casual, public contacts at a local level', writes Jacobs, 'is a feeling for the public identity of people, a web of public respect and trust, and a resource in time of personal or neighbourhood need' (1992, p. 56). This becomes particularly important in highly individualised or segregated communities and therefore has an important role to play in intergenerational and intercultural relations (Yarker, 2021).

The concept of encounter is useful here in understanding the interactions people have with those who are different from themselves precisely because of the transformational potential offered by encounter. Encounter is historically coded as a meeting of those with difference or in opposition and are about disturbance, ruptures or surprise (Wilson, 2017). This becomes central to the conceptualisation of encounter as something transformational as they offer something unexpected or destabilising. This moves social engagement between people of different backgrounds beyond a point of individual interaction and allows us to think about them more widely (Yarker, 2021).

However as a critical concept, encounter also remains open to the possibility that such engagements with difference may not always be positive and, at the very least, may have unintended consequences. Indeed, it would be naive and irresponsible not to recognise the potentially negative form that encounters can take. It is impossible to separate social encounters and the spaces in which they occur from 'the knotty issue of inequalities' (Valentine, 2008, p. 333). We must remain mindful that that encounters across difference of any type need to be *meaningful* and can only be so if they actually change values for the people involved in a positive and progressive way (Valentine, 2008).

Age-friendly programmes are often focused on increasing the opportunities for older people to have social interactions in an effort to reduce their risk of social isolation. This is done in a diversity of ways such as supporting older people to attend social groups and activities or to participate in volunteering. Evaluations of such interventions are patchy, but there is a normative assumption that any social interaction is helpful for reducing social isolation and indeed the discussion above has argued for a broadening out of what we understand by 'interaction'. Very little attention, however, is given to how these different types of interactions might lead to different types of social relationships or the uses that these different social relationships might have for older people. More discretion is needed in considering how different spaces of social infrastructure might facilitate different types of social relationships and the importance of these for age-friendly communities. To understand the varying types of social relationships that are supported by social infrastructure, we now turn to a discussion of the concept of social capital.

Social Capital

Social capital is a widely used (and many would argue abused) concept in the social sciences that has also gained considerable traction within social policy debate. Essentially social capital is a way of understanding our social relationships, connections and networks. Just as we might have economic capital in the form of money and assets, we also have social capital in the form of relationships and connections. Economic capital has certain uses such as allowing us to be able to purchase goods and services, providing us with a certain level of security and, in some cases, giving us a certain social status. Social capital has uses also. We can use our social capital to access practical support like having friends to help us move house or emotional support when dealing with difficult life events. We can also use our social capital to gain information and advice such as when looking for jobs, for example.

As a concept, social capital also helps us differentiate between the types of social relationships that we have and to understand what the different uses of these relationships. It is a concept with a very long history and a substantial amount of debate around its meaning and use. It is not the intention of this chapter to provide an account of those debates; however, it will outline the different types of social capital so as to give us an understanding of the different types of social relationships that can be produced within social infrastructure.

There are various definitions and conceptualisations of social capital (see Schuller, 2007); however, the understanding that has become most incorporated into social policy is the work of Robert Putnam (1993a, 1993b, 2000). This is a conceptualisation that is combined with notions of civil society where voluntary and non-government associations are credited as the institutions that generate social capital. Put very simply, Putnam viewed a lack of measurable civil society activity as indicative of a lack of social capital with his now well-rehearsed analogy of US citizens preferring to bowl alone rather than belong to organised associations and groups.

Social scientists emphasise two main dimensions of social capital; bonding and bridging capital also referred to as social glue and social bridges. Bonding capital refers to the social ties that connect individuals and groups who have some shared commonality such as people with a shared religious faith. Bridging capital is the links between different groups that act as bridges into the larger social world outside of their own such as intercultural or inter-generational connections. As well as the type of social connections people have, we can also use the concept of social capital to distinguish between the strength and depth of relationships. Granovetter's (1973) work distinguishes between strong ties (frequent contacts and deep emotional involvement) and weak ties (acquaintances with sporadic interactions and low emotional commitment) and makes the argument that it is these weak ties that provide essential links between different social networks. The importance of these weak ties is that they can be used to circulate information from people in different networks; 'removing a weak tie, therefore, could potentially cause far more damage to transmission of knowledge than the elimination of a strong tie' (Hauser, Tappeiner, & Walde, 2007, p. 77). A focus on ties highlights the importance of networks to the conceptualisation of social capital. Some researchers who engage with the concept place a greater emphasis on the role of networks rather than other dimensions such as trust or reciprocity (Halpern, 2005; Foley and Edwards – in; Naughton, 2014). In having a better appreciation of the different dimensions of social capital and the ways in which they work together, Halpern's (2005) use of Warr's (1987) vitamin model is helpful in drawing attention to how we need different types of social capital (bridging and bonding, weak and strong ties) for a healthy and effective society and that, just as with vitamins, too much of one or too little of another can lead to deficiencies and imbalances.

Within social policy literature, there is a generalised understanding that social capital is produced within institutions and civil society organisations. Very little of this discussion, however, goes far enough in adequality theorising how different dimensions of social capital might be produced to varying degrees in different types of social and institutional spaces. The question we therefore need to ask is which types of spaces are useful in producing which types of social capital? We need a more context-specific understanding of social capital, one that would focus on its diverse contexts and processes and thereby allowing it to be conceptualised as an emergent effect of social relationships (Naughton, 2014). This spatially sensitive starting point would allow us to question how social networks are established and how space, place and materiality affects these processes.

SOCIAL INFRASTRUCTURE AND AGE-FRIENDLY COMMUNITIES

So how can an infrastructural approach and an understanding of the different types of social capital be applied to the study of age-friendly work and communities? As we saw in the introduction, an important aspect of age-friendly communities is that they are a place where older people feel connected to those around them and to the community in which they live. It is also a place where older people feel empowered to be actively engaged in their communities and are supported in doing so. The importance of social relationships and networks for older people is a well-established area of research and policy debate. However, what is lacking from these discussions is a detailed understanding of the role space plays in shaping the types of interactions that older people have in their communities. Therefore, taking an infrastructural approach to the study of age-friendly communities allows us to think not just about the importance of specific social connections for older people but also draws our attention to the different types of spaces that may be needed for these connections to develop. Crucially, an infrastructural approach forces us to think holistically when it comes to older people and the places they use for social interaction, considering a diversity of spaces to reflect the diversity of the ageing population. Throughout this book, it will be argued that older people need a diversity of different types of social connections; they need strong close friendships just as much as they need casual acquittances and to recognise familiar faces in their neighbourhoods. Therefore, we need a diversity of social infrastructure to support these different needs.

Our understanding of sources of social support for older people has shifted in recent years from a focus solely on families and towards the role of 'personal communities' such as friends and neighbours (Phillipson et al., 2001). The social support of older people now considers a wider array of actors all taking on a more prominent role in the social networks of older people. Gray (2009) found that neighbourhood contacts actually have a greater effect in providing support for older people than being active, having a partner or having had children. Scharf and De Jong Gierveld (2008) concluded that having wider community-focused networks led to older people reporting lower levels of loneliness than those with more private and restricted networks.

Such community networks have been conceptualised as 'natural neighbourhood networks' by Gardner (2011) in her study of the social networks of older adults. In this study, she categorised the different types of relationships important to older people. The first type of relationship she identifies are *relationships of proximity*, such as those between immediate neighbours or 'regulars' in specific neighbourhood place such as a café, for example. Secondly, there are *relationships of service* such as those working within various parts of our social infrastructure (shop assistants, cashiers, librarians, etc.) and thirdly *relationships of chance* meaning the strangers we come into contact with in third places. Gardner's work helps to identify and animate the wider array of actors involved in the social networks of older people and encourages us to look outside of the immediate personal networks of an individual and consider the host of other actors we come into contact within during our everyday lives in a community.

The typology also draws closer attention to exactly what the multiple benefits of these interactions might be. For example, relationships of service with people such as shop assistants or bus drivers were found to be important to older people because they were about being recognised and valued in public spaces. Research has previously highlighted that older people can often feel invisible in public spaces so the positive interactions they had with shop assistants and the like often provided a sense of validation which is important in feeling a sense of connection and belonging to where you live. Relationships of proximity (i.e. with neighbours) and of chance were more closely related to having a sense of security and of mutual support. Crucially, however, relationships of chance were important because they instilled a sense of familiarity and recognition but without associated feelings of obligation or need for commitment. They reflect, therefore, the importance of weak ties of association discussed by Granovetter (1973) and the importance of social ties that require minimal effort or maintenance.

Gardner's work is also useful because it categorises the different spaces in a community in which these different types of relationships can be developed. She distinguishes between third places and transitory zones, for example. Drawing on the work of Oldenburg (1989), third places are described by Gardner as the key sites in a community where informal public life takes place. This mainly refers to destination space such as parks, coffee shops, markets and libraries. Transitory zones, on the other hand, are not destinations but are the places we pass through during the course of daily public life. Gardner also identifies the importance of threshold spaces for older people. This refers to semi-public or hybrid spaces such as balconies, lobbies, private gardens or backyards that although are not accessible to the wider public do, nonetheless, offer opportunity for social interaction, mostly with immediate neighbours. Especially when it comes to age-friendly communities, it is important that we think beyond the types of spaces we might more readily associate with older people such as community centres and spaces related to age-specific activities or services.

There are two points upon which this book wishes to extend Gardner's work on natural neighbourhood networks. The first is to take the different types of relationships she identifies and be more specific about *how* these relationships are important for older people. For this, we draw upon the concept of social capital (discussed above) to differentiate between bridging and bonding capital but also to explore the strength of these relationships through Granovetter's work on weak ties of association. The second is to further conceptualise Gardner's typology of spaces through a theoretical framework of social infrastructure. This book offers the distinction of passing places and destination places to distinguish between the different types of social infrastructure and to argue that it is just as important to have social infrastructure that acts as passing place, where people can have fleeting social interactions, as it is to have destination spaces where people have the opportunity to develop more substantial relationships and strong bonds. Passing places are not just confined to the transitory zones identified by Gardner above. They can also be spaces where we can have passing interactions. For example, a post office might not be a destination for social interaction, but it can provide a space where people pass by one another and have some form of social encounter. Equally, a park might be a destination to meet with a friend or a volunteer group, but it might also be a passing place for regular exercisers or dog walkers. This furthers the spatial analysis by providing a way to understand how particular spaces can lend themselves to producing and supporting certain types of social interaction and therefore relationships.

THE DIVERSITY OF SOCIAL INFRASTRUCTURE

The next three chapters have an ambitious task. They seek to bring together a diverse set of literatures, research studies and reports to see what we can learn from existing research about how different types of social infrastructures might contribute to creating age-friendly communities. The task is an ambitious one because, as we have already noted, the concept of social infrastructure can be applied to a diversity of different spaces. It is beyond the scope of this book to cover the literature on each and every place. Therefore, we start by classifying social infrastructures into different categories and discussing a handful of examples to illustrate each one. In doing this, the discussions draw on literatures from gerontology, sociology, human geography, community studies, marketing, communication and leisure studies. The research discussed offers empirically rich examples of the types of spaces we are interested in, and therefore the few select examples provide an illustration of how different types of infrastructure can support older people and age-friendly communities.

So how might we begin to categorise the different types of social infrastructures? Jeffres, Bracken, Jian, and Casey (2009) offer a useful typology of spaces based on a national US-based survey where they asked respondents to identify third places in their communities. Jeffres work groups important third places into four categories. The first they define as places of 'Eating, drinking and Talking'; this would include pubs, cafes, restaurants, etc., places that people tend to visit socially, as part of their leisure time and that often includes the co-ordination with other people. They separate this from 'Commercial Venues' which would include shops, markets, shopping centres, post offices and beauty salons. The third category they found was 'Outside Venues' which include parks, waterfronts, public squares and the space of the high street itself and their final category 'Organised Activities' such as places of worship, community centres and leisure centres. These categories offer a useful starting point from which to start discussing the different types of social infrastructures and the different roles they can play in supporting the social connections of older people. This book, however, suggests one additional category of 'Public Services and Institutions'. This would include public transport but also public libraries and medical centres, schools and universities. Such sites can sometimes be thought of alongside commercial establishments, but there are important differences in the regularity in which they are used, the motivation for using them, the activities they host as well as the potential economic and cultural barriers more commonly found with commercial sites.

Therefore, drawing on and extending Jeffres et al. (2009) typology of third places, the following chapters are organised as follows;

- Chapter 3 looks at *outside venues and public spaces* which includes various types of green and non-green public spaces alongside a discussion of what it means for a space to be 'public' or 'semi-public'.

- Chapter 4 considers *organised activities and public institutions.* This is the longest of the chapters and considers venues and organisations that bring groups of people together including faith-based organisations, public libraries, schools and the community and voluntary sector.

- Chapter 5 discusses *commercial enterprises* that might be considered social infrastructures covering both retail spaces and hospitality venues, drawing on Jeffres et al. (2009) category of 'Eating, drinking and socialising'.

In discussing the research examples for each category of social infrastructure, this book will consider the two main ways that these spaces can support older people living in communities. Firstly, in how they provide opportunities to have social interactions and develop social connections and secondly, in how these spaces might contribute to a broader sense of community cohesion from which older people especially can benefit. The following three chapters consider how different types of social infrastructure might contribute to both these aspects of age-friendly communities.

By taking an infrastructural approach to age-friendly communities, we are able to focus more directly on what types of spaces we need to create and invest in that can support social interactions for older people. It encourages us to take a broad interpretation of what social infrastructure is and to think beyond the types of social spaces that typically come to mind. Specifically, this book argues that thinking infrastructurally encourages us to think about the seemingly naturally occurring mundane interactions that take place in community third places that may or may not have a primary social focus as well as thinking beyond spaces that are typically associated with one age group, such as nurseries and sheltered accommodation. Here we are thinking of places such as shops, cafes, public transport and green space, spaces used by all age groups, albeit in perhaps in different ways. Places that are defined by their ordinariness and unassuming nature (Finlay, Esposito, Hee Kim, Gomez-Lopez, & Clarke, 2019). What will hopefully become apparent throughout the book is that one type of social interaction is not necessarily better or more favourable than another. What we will see from the examples from existing literature is that different types of social interaction produce different types of social relationships and that all have their uses in different ways and in different contexts.

3

OUTSIDE VENUES AND PUBLIC SPACES

Social infrastructures that can be considered as outside venues include any type of public green space, such as parks, nature reserves and community gardens, as well as non-green public spaces such as squares, plazas and, in some instances, public spaces around retail and leisure quarters and high streets. It can also refer to some semi-private spaces such as communal gardens and lobbies. Some of these spaces can also be thought of as transitional spaces, spaces that are used to get somewhere or as open spaces, i.e., they have no pre-designed purpose. This chapter separates out the literature on green and non-green public space although there are considerable overlaps especially when it comes to thinking about how these types of social infrastructures might be improved for older people.

PUBLIC SPACE

Definitions of public space vary (Briggs, 1963; Goheen, 1998; Habermas, 1989; Sennett, 1974) and, therefore, so too does the focus of studies in this area. Some studies concentrate on spaces that are open to the public, but that might be privately owned, such as shopping centres or public squares within retail or office developments. Other spaces that have been studied under the theme of public space are those places that might be considered 'semi-public' such as communal gardens, balconies and stairwells in apartment buildings (see Gardner, 2011). What unites all these different spaces, however, is that they are spaces that we use in the course of our everyday lives. They are not often destination spaces (although they may be at times) but spaces that are passed through, used to get elsewhere or used because they are the sites of other venues such as a shopping mall or a high street.

Worpole and Knox (2007) argue we need to go beyond the traditional definition of public space often used in design policy which hinges on an identification of ownership. In their review of the social value of public space, they found that:

> To members of the public, it is not the ownership of places or their appearance that makes them 'public', but their shared use for a diverse range of activities by a range of different people.
>
> (p. 4)

This means that despite the important implications of ownership (in terms of security, exclusivity and access) what is most important for the purposes of analysing the social relations in a place is how people perceive and appropriate that space.

There has been much debate in urban studies in recent decades around the privatisation of 'public' space. In reality very little 'public' space has ever truly been public. Most spaces are owned by someone. In most cases, what we understand as public spaces in our everyday lives will be owned by local authorities but increasingly the ownership and/or the management of such spaces is transferred to private owners such as property developers. This has produced what many refer to as 'public–private' spaces, spaces that might appear public in nature but are actually privately owned and managed accordingly. Anna Minton (2006) has written extensively on this issue of 'public–private' spaces and points to a 'quiet revolution' (p. 10) taking place in the United Kingdom as public spaces previously owned by local authorities are being sold to private developers.

Despite a difficulty in obtaining exact figures to quantify this shift in ownership, Minton raises important concerns around the impacts of countries such as the UK 'sleepwalking (their) way to a privatisation of the public realm' (p. 23). She points to the rise in public–private spaces as one contributing factor, amongst many, in the 'breakdown' of community. She argues public–private spaces produce 'over-controlled, sterile places (that) lack connection to the reality and diversity of the local environment'. This can serve to reinforce divisions between social groups characterised as 'different' from one another by removing or limiting the opportunities for local populations to mix and have informal interactions with one another. For Minton, this 'underpins the trend towards the creation of individual neighbourhoods of atomised communities' (Minton, 2006, p. 23). This has important implications for community cohesion.

With changes in the ownership of public space comes a change in the management and, therefore, the security of public space. Minton (2006) has written critically of the use of private security firms used to 'police' public space arguing that the broad range of powers private security firms have over such spaces focus too much on an anti-social behaviour agenda, mirroring zero tolerance approaches of policing. This, Minton continues, serves to criminalise non-criminal behaviour in a public space such as being homeless, riding a skateboard or putting up posters, and contributes to the alienating of these spaces from the surrounding local community and the excluding of certain people and practices.

There is also evidence of self-exclusion from public spaces which means certain groups of people self-regulating how and when they use a space in a way which feels comfortable to them. For example, research on older people's use of public space has observed quite different patterns of use compared to younger people. Holland, Clark, Katz, and Peace (2017) study of the use of public space in the town of Aylesbury in the United Kingdom observed that older people were more likely to use public space during the morning, visiting either alone or in pairs, and were far less likely to visit public spaces after dark. This corroborates research by Pain (2001) which found some older people, especially women, were fearful of using public spaces after dark. This is important because being able to access a space is about far more than just using it. It is about claiming a right to use that space and being visible in the public domain, the community and wider society. This is especially important for groups which may experience wider discrimination or social exclusion.

The result of centring policy discussions about public space around questions of anti-social behaviour, disorder and securitisation are efforts to 'design out' 'problems' in public spaces. Much less is known, however, about what makes a public space a sociable one and much less policy-orientated research has focused on the social value of public space and the wider societal benefits it can bring.

In their report on Inclusive Healthy Places (2018), the Gehl Institute demonstrates the social value of inclusive public spaces by highlighting the positive relationship between public space, levels of trust and collective action. They argue that spaces which are accessible to a diversity of people can increase tolerance and empathy towards others. Higher levels of trust in a community can provide the foundation for collective and civic action with research showing that even living near a public park or other public space that is both popular and used can lead to higher levels of civic trust. 'The trust of a city street' argues Jane Jacobs (1992) 'is formed over time from many, many, little public sidewalk (sic) contacts' (p. 56). When spaces are well used and by a diversity of people, they can create a 'feel-good' buzz from being around a busy environment. It allows people to display their cultural identities, develop an awareness of diversity and difference, have social interactions and create local attachments (Worpole & Knox, 2007).

Many public spaces can be characterised as passing places, where people pass by one another in temporary and unchoreographed ways and, therefore, the types of social interactions that occur between strangers in public spaces are usually informal and unplanned. Holland et al. (2017) note a lack of what they refer to as 'real' interactions between people of different ages in public space. By this they meant they didn't observe older and younger people conversing with each other in what they would define as a meaningful way. They did, however, note examples of strangers holding doors open for one another, offering seats and helping older people up if they had a stumble or a fall. These interactions might be functional and largely superficial, but to dismiss them as unmeaningful is to miss their potential to make incremental differences over time. These acts are examples of low-level sociability which, as Holland et al. go on to discuss, involve an 'underlying orderliness by which people avoid conflict and sometimes feel a sense of belonging' (p. 64). So as much as these interactions might not be very substantial in themselves, they are nonetheless important for societal and community cohesion.

These types of weak interactions can be highly valued by older people. In their study of older people's neighbourhood interactions in the Netherlands, Lager, Van Hoven, and Huigen (2013) found even passing interactions gave them a sense of security that people in the neighbourhood were 'watching out' for one another without any overbearing obligations or responsibilities. Lager et al. also observed that social contact does not always have to be through verbal communication. The older people in their study placed great value on visual and audio encounters with others in their neighbourhood. Being able to see and hear children playing in the streets, for example, or being aware of the general everyday life of the neighbourhood from their windows enabled older people to retain a sense of connection to place. The importance of visual links to the neighbourhood and non-obligatory willingness to offer practical and emotional support to neighbours have also been borne out by research into the neighbourhood impacts for people living with dementia (Ward et al., 2018).

The literature on public space is often keen to emphasise the importance of good quality public space. What counts as 'good quality', however, is often subject for debate as some research has argued that over-planned spaces with *too much* emphasis on design can actually design out the types of spontaneous and informal uses of public space that are so valuable and that it is often the more informal, less tidy and unassuming public spaces that can be of great importance to a local community (Worpole & Knox, 2007). There is, however, some agreement on some of the features of public space that should be championed. Facilities such as benches, street furniture and toilets have been found to be very important, especially in age-friendly design, as has the provision of shade and shelter from the weather (Gehl Institute, 2018). Many of these features have also been found to be important in green space which will be discussed next.

GREEN SPACE

The positive impact of access to parks and other green spaces for the well-being of urban residents is clearly evidenced (Bedimo-Rung, Mowen, & Cohen, 2005; Kaczynski & Henderson, 2007). This is especially the case for older people who, due to limited mobility or resources, may be more bound to their neighbourhoods. For older people, having access to green spaces in their living environment has been shown to decrease feelings of loneliness and increase sources of social support through opportunities to develop social ties (Bedimo-Rung, Mowen, & Cohen, 2005; Maas, Dillen van, Verheij, & Groenewegen, 2009). An expansive definition of green space is useful for this discussion, one which includes parks of any size, open green spaces such as woodlands, nature areas, riverside and commons, as well as community gardens and allotments. As this is a discussion around green space as social infrastructure, private gardens are not included. Whilst there are no doubts that gardens are incredibly important to the well-being of those who have them, being private property and not a public meeting place, private gardens do not meet our definition of social infrastructure and, therefore, will not be included in this discussion.

A recent study of green infrastructure in Greater Manchester, UK, identified four main benefits green spaces bring to older people (GHIA, 2019). The first was that these places acted as markers of important biographical events and memories. This use of memory landscape was first identified by the influential writer on ageing, Rowles (1983), in his discussions of how older people use certain features of places to maintain a sense of continuity and biographical 'insiderness' as they age. Second, the study found that green spaces were important in providing opportunities for connecting with nature and volunteering alongside others. This supports growing evidence of the importance of volunteering to older people in later life, particularly when this volunteering involves green spaces and nature. There is also a growing awareness of the importance of green space for the mental, as well as physical health, of older people. Third, green spaces were found to provide vital opportunities for older people to be active outdoors and finally, and of most interest for this book, the GHIA study supported the argument that green spaces provide opportunities for older people to develop and maintain social relationships, independence and personal growth.

So, what are the different types of green spaces that make up our social infrastructure and how might they support the social connections of older people? Much of the literature on the use of green space by older people is based on case study research in the United States or Australia (Macintyre et al., 2019). This means there are important climatic and cultural differences to consider when trying to relate these research findings to other national contexts. These studies also tend to focus on larger green spaces and bigger public parks. However, research based in the United Kingdom from Macintyre et al. looked exclusively at how older people used smaller urban green spaces in and around their neighbourhoods. They found that their participants rarely perceived these small green spaces as 'theirs', instead of viewing them as spaces for families and the households that lived immediately nearby. Older people in this study preferred to visit larger parks because they felt more public and inclusive.

Whilst many studies have documented how people use parks and the types of activities that take place in them, few studies have looked in detail at the types of social interactions that actually take place. One exception is Peters, Elands, and Buijs (2010) study of the social interactions of different groups of people in Dutch parks. They looked in close detail at how park users interacted with each other and found that most interactions between strangers were limited to brief conversations usually related to specific issues such as children, dogs or the weather. They also identified high amounts of non-verbal interactions such as people-watching and general hanging around. Despite the passive and superficial nature of much of these interactions, interviews with park users found they were still very much valued and that parks were seen by many as opportunities for interaction. This supports the arguments made above in relation to public (non-green) spaces that the value of these fleeting interactions that occur in these passing places should not be underestimated.

Parks and other green spaces in neighbourhoods can also be host to more formal social participation. For example, the 'Friends of' voluntary movement seen across the United Kingdom offers opportunities for people of all ages to engage in gardening-related activities, and many health and social care programmes will utilise available green space to provide outdoor activities for older people. Studies of physical exercise programmes utilising parks that are aimed at older people show that it is not just the physical activity that older people enjoy but also the opportunity for socialising.

Parks are typical third places for Oldenburg as they are locally accessible and open to all at extended times of the day. Therefore, a park will be used by a diversity of local residents and visitors albeit in differing ways. For Jane Jacobs (1992), this diversity of use is vital in supporting the vibrancy of urban areas and, in turn, sustaining busier public places with more likelihood of social contact. It is this diversity of use that is also important for the development of bridging capital. For example, Neal, Bennett, Jones, Cochrane, and Mohan (2015) suggest that parks in highly diverse areas are important for the convivial encounter across ethnic and cultural difference. The opportunities provided by parks for older people from different cultural backgrounds to develop even weak social ties with others can be crucial for maintaining a sense of connection to local areas in later life.

Allotments and community gardens offer a more private experience of green space than public parks, with some membership or ownership needed to gain access; however, depending on how they are organised, they can still be important shared community spaces. Studies of organised group activities that occur in allotments and community gardens showed the importance of the social networks that develop from them for group members (Genter, Roberts, Richardson, & Sheaff, 2015). Milligan, Gatrell, and Bingley (2004) found that communal gardening on allotments has social and well-being benefits that can be particularly important for older people. Loss of physical and/cognitive capacity as we age can make maintaining a private garden unmanageable. In addition, moving home in later life may result in the loss of one's private garden. Indeed, those living in flats or on low incomes may not have had access to a garden at all. In these instances, Milligan et al. argue communal allotment gardening offers an inclusive, safe space where older people can garden in a mutually supportive environment. Their study, based in Northern England, concluded that communal allotment gardening was able to combat social isolation and contributed to the development of social networks. Studies of solo allotment gardening, however, show that there is less of an emphasis placed on social interaction. Indeed, a survey of allotment gardening by Van den Berg et al. (2010) found social contact was only rated as very important by 17% of respondents of all ages. This did, however, increase slightly for the over 60s age group in the sample. The variation in these studies shows that it is not just the presence of social infrastructures that is important, but how they are managed, and the activities that take place within them. The presence of allotments in a community provides a space of social infrastructure only for those older people who own them unless there is a programme of communal or group activity running within them.

Community gardens, on the other hand, as is suggested by the name, have been found to have a much greater capacity for facilitating social interactions and community cohesion. Draper and Freedman (2010) argued that the collective nature of gardening can lead to meaningful social interactions particularly between 'strangers' as gardening tasks provide the impetus for informal conversations. In a study of community gardens in Australia, Dolley (2020) identified exchanges of gardening knowledge, the sharing of tools, conversations about the weather and other topics related to gardening, all facilitated informal interactions between relative strangers. Although informal and perhaps lacking in substance, these interactions were found to provide the basis of connections both between the individuals but also with the wider community. Dolley points to the potential of community gardens for reducing social isolation as a result. Indeed, the social interactions that occur in parks and other green space have been found to have wider implications than the social connections of the individual. Studies have found that even the fleeting and cursory interactions that occur in these spaces can be the building blocks of community cohesion. This is especially important in highly diverse and potentially segregated neighbourhoods where public green space can be an important site of encounter with difference.

This can occur in a number of ways. Firstly, simply seeing people on a regular basis can lead to greater levels of familiarity with one another (Peters et al., 2010). Being around people to mingle and have informal interactions can bring what Lofland calls 'a momentary glow of fellow feeling' (1998, p. 39), something especially important to those who live alone or who are socially isolated. In addition, several studies of the use public green spaces have shown how they are able to give people a sense of belonging or attachment to a place, and researchers have shown that levels of place attachment positively correlate with levels of social cohesion (Forrest & Kearns, 2001). For example, in a study of community gardening in St Luis, Shinew, Glover, and Parry (2004) found that gardeners perceived a sense of connection to their community garden and, through this, a connection to the other gardeners. This sense of connection and attachment can help nurture a sense of commitment to a place (Dines & Cattell, 2006; Yarker, 2019). Therefore, the feelings of belonging, social support and commitment to a place that are cultivated through the use of public spaces such as parks can create a sense of togetherness with other park users leading to higher levels of familiarity, trust and ultimately community cohesion. Exploring how urban green spaces support social interactions and social cohesion can inform strategies to improve urban health (Jennings & Bamkole, 2019) as well as ageing in place and policies for age-friendly communities.

So, what makes a 'good quality' green space for older people? The question of proximity versus quality of green space divide's opinion within the literature. Some studies argue that living close to green space, particularly being within walking distance is the most important for older people. This would appear to make sense in the context of older people often being less mobile and more tied to their local communities. It would also align with Oldenburg's stipulation that third places need to be 'local' and 'walkable'. However, other studies have found that the importance of proximity of green space is outweighed if they are not perceived as safe, accessible and of good quality. Perceived safety remains a significant challenge in maximising the benefits of green space for older people (Hong et al., 2018). This is not just an issue for parks themselves but also for the wider surrounding neighbourhood. Older people need to feel safe as pedestrians at all times of the day and night before we can confidently say a place is age-friendly.

Ward Thompson (2013) concluded from her research that green spaces must be well managed and include facilities such as high-quality paths, benches and toilets if they are to be amenable to older people. Local parks must also be perceived as safe places if older people are to visit them (Kazmierczak, 2013). The reverse of this is that poorly maintained parks and other green spaces can actually discourage positive social behaviour (Bedimo-Rung et al., 2005). This has also been found to be the case for non-green, or 'hard' spaces such as streets, markets and public squares (Dines & Cattell, 2006) with a vast literature in environmental psychology demonstrating that it is the quality of public space, not merely the existence of it, that has the most impact on encouraging sociability. Quality features and focal points, such as public art, food outlets, connected pathways and seating, have been identified as influencing social interaction in public space (Bedimo-Rung et al., 2005). Veitch, Flowers, Ball, Deforche, and Timperio (2020) conducted walk-along interviews with participants aged 65 years and over in several parks in Melbourne, Australia, to try to identify the qualities of green spaces that made them age-friendly. They found that older people were more likely to use parks that were well maintained, peaceful, were attractive environments with established trees, gardens and birdlife, seating provision, pleasant paths, toilets, cafes, water features, shade and shelter from the elements, facilities for grandchildren and the presence of other people. Several features of green spaces were identified that were particularly valued by older people for facilitating social interaction, and these included the provision of picnic and BBQ areas, organised events and cafes.

PASSING PLACES FOR INTERACTIONS WITH DIVERSITY

The value of green spaces and other public spaces to the social life of our communities is that they are accessible to all, representing true third places according to Oldenburg and Bissett (1982). They are able to draw in a diversity of people from across the community and offer the opportunity for meaningful encounters with difference. Jane Jacobs in her seminal book *The Death and Life of Great American Cities* (1992) argued that diversity in public spaces was crucial for the social economy of cities and that one of the most important conditions for diversity was that city infrastructures must serve more than one primary function. This means that parks and public spaces must ensure the presence of people who are using the space for different purposes and at varying times of the day. This increases the potential to have encounters with difference.

Such encounters, although often based initially on weak ties of association and passing, sometimes non-verbal interactions, can nonetheless be the starting point for greater community cohesion and can help to sustain the age-friendliness of neighbourhoods. These are passing places with no barrier to entry and open to a diversity of people. In theory therefore, these types of outside venues should be able to facilitate the development of bridging social capital between individuals and groups of different backgrounds. However, these are spaces which are increasingly subject to changes in their ownership, management and, therefore, surveillance which can socially exclude particular groups and inhibit the types of informal social interactions that weak ties of bridging capital can be dependent upon. Therefore, age-friendly work must ensure that age-friendly principles of inclusivity and accessibility in their broadest understandings are maintained in our public spaces.

4

ORGANISED ACTIVITY, PUBLIC SERVICES AND INSTITUTIONS

The typology of third places offered by Jeffres, Bracken, Jian, and Casey (2009) identifies a category they call 'organised activity'. For this reason, this chapter will begin with a discussion of some of the existing research around different types of organised activities and how they can support the social connections of older people. However, where this discussion departs from Jeffres et al. is with the inclusion of 'public services and institutions' as a separate category. Whilst social infrastructures of organised activity and public services have much in common, there are also important differences requiring them to be thought of separately.

ORGANISED ACTIVITY

Organised activities are group and social activities that include 'churches, clubs, and organisations, community centres and meetings, and senior centres' (Jeffres et al., 2009, p. 338). This is a very useful category, especially in the field of ageing studies as it tends to reflect many of the social interventions around loneliness and isolation for older people. In this chapter, we will consider the role of the community and voluntary sector (also referred to as the third sector), the role of religious organisations and group leisure activities.

Community and Voluntary Sector

The community and voluntary sector plays a crucial role in providing opportunities for social interaction for older people as well as vulnerable or marginalised groups in our communities. However, the ways in which the third sector operates in communities vary, so the discussion in this chapter will consider the role of day centres, volunteering opportunities as well as activities and groups organised by the voluntary sector.

The role of the community and voluntary sector in high-income economies has changed substantially in recent decades. It has moved from having a mainly small and discreet role to becoming 'the shadow state' (Wolch, 1989) as more services provided by the welfare state have become the business of the third sector. The expansion of the third sector into public service delivery means an increasing number of people are coming into contact with third sector organisations on a daily basis, and the organisations and services that make up the sector locally are becoming a more important part of our social infrastructure for a greater diversity of people. Older people in particular, spending more time in their local neighbourhoods, are often key stakeholders within the sector, as user of its services, as participants in organised groups and activities and as volunteers within organisations.

The shifting landscape of voluntarism in the United Kingdom in particular has led to what Conradson (2003) has termed a new contemporary landscape of care. The third sector has always, by its very nature, been involved in the provision of care for community residents, but over recent decades these once informal arrangements have become increasingly formalised through shifts in government policy. In the United Kingdom, the 2014 Care Act stipulated that all local authorities should work in partnership with the third sector to develop 'a vibrant, responsive market of service provision' (DH, 2016, papa 4.1, quoted in Abendstern, Hughes, Jasper, Sutcliffe, & Challis, 2018, p. 315). Much of the newly formalised provision and co-ordination of care by the third sector has focused on older adults. Therefore, as well as becoming important sites of health care, the community and voluntary organisations involved have also become important parts of the social infrastructure for older users as well. However, in their review of research into the involvement of the third sector in care co-ordination in the United Kingdom, Abendstern et al. concluded there was a significant gap in the research that looked at how older people experienced these settings, so it is difficult to say with any certainty what the social impacts of these new spaces of care might be.

Research on older people's social networks have increasing looked outside of the family unit towards 'personal communities' (Pahl & Spencer, 2004) defined as networks of support which are less kin-based and more orientated towards friends and neighbours. Adding to this, work on age-friendly communities continues to provide evidence to support the importance of having opportunities for civil participation, and voluntary organisations play a large part in providing these opportunities. For those older people living on low incomes and in more economically marginalised communities, their contact with community organisations may be one of the only times they have social interactions outside of the family and for those who are living alone or without relatives nearby, they might be the only form of social contact they have. However, many large-scale studies of social participation in later life tend to include engagement with community groups, sports, leisure and religious organisations together under a category of 'organised activity'. Although this is helpful in some respects, this makes it difficult to distinguish between the different types of social connections that might be made by attending a church, for example, compared to a community-based craft group. What we do know, however, is that any type of community-based activity can bring huge benefits to older people in increasing their social networks, reducing social isolation and fostering a sense of connection to the communities in which they live. We also know that shared spaces that draw in a diversity of people are useful in supporting the development of bridging capital between users, so community organisations that cater to a range of different groups will have this potential. Equally spaces that encourage informal interactions and conversation can support weak ties, and spaces that bring together people with a shared background or experience can create strong bonding capital. Therefore, considering the diversity of community and voluntary organisations and the services and activities they offer, we can conclude that they are vital parts of social infrastructure for older people, offering the potential to develop a range of different types of social connections.

Day Centres

Day centres are 'community-based services that provide care and/or health related services and/or activities specifically for older people who are disabled and/or in need' (Orellana, Manthorpe, & Tinker, 2020a, p. 2) and, therefore, form a key part of social infrastructure for age-friendly communities. In the United Kingdom, such centres are provided by local authorities in conjunction with the third sector with the aim of supporting older people to remain living in their own homes and neighbourhoods. As places for older people to visit on a regular basis their potential as spaces of social interaction is great, however limited research exists on users' experiences. What we do know, however, is that they provide valuable spaces for the most vulnerable older people and those most at risk of social isolation. Research has found day centre attendees tend to live alone and experience some level of restricted mobility and/or a limiting health condition. There is also a suggestion that attendees tend to be older, with one study identifying an average age of 83 (Orellana, Manthorpe, & Tinker, 2020b).

Users of day centres are motivated by wanting some level of social contact, and existing research seems to suggest this is mostly achieved. However, what we are less sure about are the types of social interactions that occur in day centres and the types of social relationships that might develop from this. There is some suggestion from Orellana et al.'s research that, through the regular interactions in day centres, users develop friendships that are quite context specific, i.e., that they are based on spending time together at the centre itself but that people do not tend to meet each other outside to socialise. This suggests these relationships might be based on weak social ties, as they do not require much in the way of maintenance but are nonetheless important for reducing social isolation and providing social support.

Research conducted in the United Kingdom by Orellana et al. (2020b) found that reasons for older people attending day centres usually related to having experienced some form of loss and was motivated by a desire for something different in life. The experience of loss, through bereavement, illness or loss of existing social networks, may provide some shared experience or commonality between users that might suggest the potential for bonding capital to develop between individuals. However, despite attendees sharing some common characteristics, it is important to remember they will not be a homogenous group (Orellana et al., 2020b), and, therefore, day centres may still attract older people from varying backgrounds depending on the demographics of the neighbourhoods they are located in. Other outcomes identified in research on day centres suggest some development in bridging capital, such as an increased inclination to become involved in other activities outside of the centre or in taking up volunteering. However, as important as they appear to be for those using them, day centres can often suffer something of an image problem, with many members of over 60 population viewing them as something 'for older people' and, therefore, not for them, preferring instead to attend organised activities that are not directly promoted as being 'for older people'. There might be a question mark, therefore, over the continued relevance of traditional day centres for future generations.

Volunteering

Volunteering provides a different example of the ways in which older people can become involved with organised activities in the voluntary sector. Active ageing policies have often focused on volunteering as a key method through which to encourage older people to remain both physically active and engaged in their communities. A wealth of research evidence points to the health and well-being benefits of volunteering in later life. These include improvements in physical health, life satisfaction, employability, skills, and feeling useful and valuable (Jopling & Jones, 2018). One of the main benefits is how volunteering can develop the social capital of older people. Promoted as a way of countering social isolation, meeting new people and building new social connections is often reported as a key benefit of volunteering by older people themselves. Qualitative studies, however, have delved deeper into the types and qualities of the social connections made through volunteering and provide useful insights when it comes to thinking about how we can support people to age in place. Research into the different types of volunteer activities older people were involved with in rural Wales found that often people were not looking to make strong social connections of friendship from their volunteering with participants stating that they already had plenty of close friendships from other aspects of their lives. Instead, what they appreciated from their volunteering was the chance to meet others from different walks of life to themselves. These interactions were often experienced as weak ties but were nonetheless important in themselves in providing pleasant social interactions whilst they were volunteering but without the obligation or responsibility to maintain the relationship outside of the volunteering context (Heley, Jones, & Yarker, 2020). Of course, this is not to say that strong friendships do not develop from sharing volunteering activities, they often can and do; however it is important to be attentive to the different types of social motivations older people might have in volunteering, and that the persuasion of 'making new friends' might not be as persuasive for everyone.

However, research on older people's involvement with voluntary activities tends to work within a fairy narrow definition of what volunteering is, and it is important that we recognise this does not capture the full range of contributions older people make to their communities, nor therefore their experiences of this participation. Large-scale volunteering surveys typically only collect information on what we might refer to as *formal* volunteering, i.e., volunteering with a formal organisation often including some level of training, induction and often with some level of regular commitment. Research carried out by the Centre for Ageing Better (2018) in the United Kingdom found that 'even those older people who do not take part in formal volunteering are often contributing to their communities and benefiting from the interactions this generates' (2018, p. 7). They found that the informal contributions that older people made to their communities, through actions such as doing a neighbours shopping, translating a letter for a friend or giving someone a lift to a hospital appointment, were both hugely valuable for the individual as well as being impactful for the wider community. These are all vital contributions being made to civil society, yet not always captured in large-scale research into volunteering. This also skews which older people are represented in the data and, therefore, visible as volunteers. Those older people most commonly engaged in formal volunteering tend to be the younger older age group, those who are wealthier, more highly educated and in better health. These demographics tend to map onto ethnic privilege too, with the experiences of white British volunteers being more represented within these studies.

The absence of the experiences of older people from different minority ethnic and low-income groups in volunteering research reflects some of the methodologies of the studies but does not mean these groups are not actively involved in their communities. Far from it, what it does indicate, however, is that the ways in which some older people are involved in their communities are not adequately reflected by either the term 'volunteer' or within the volunteering literature. In fact, some research has found an active resistance to the stereotype of 'volunteer' (Jopling & Jones, 2018). For others, especially those from some minority ethnic groups, making contributions to the community is typically done in a much more informal way, not always through third sector organisations but through extended family and friendship networks. Therefore, we need to be mindful that the voluntary work of many older people may not be adequately reflected in large-scale research studies and as a consequence we know less about the types of social connections made through these activities.

Religious Organisations

That religious organisations play a prominent role in the lives of their congregations is perhaps obvious. However, religious buildings, or faith-based organisations (FBOs) as they are most commonly referred to in the literature, can also be central agents of development in their wider neighbourhoods. They have close, long-standing relationships with their communities and often a better understanding of their service needs than some outside bodies. The role of FBOs as community development anchors has been formalised in recent years through third-way policies in many Western societies. This means that they can become part of wider community-based networks providing services that either the state or the market does not. They become part of the shadow state in a similar way to non-religious third sector organisations

(Wolch, 1989). Christian churches providing food banks would be a prominent example of FBOs providing a service and a contribution to the community outside its own congregation and the wider neighbourhood in which it operates.

There is a wealth of evidence of the spiritual, physical and emotional benefits brought to those who identify with a faith (Ellor, 2004; Ellor & Coates, 1986). The study of the role of religion in the lives of older people has an entire academic journal dedicated to it, *The Journal of Religion, Spirituality and Aging,* yet Fields, Adorno, Magruder, Parekh, and Felderhoff (2016) note (in a paper in this very journal) that the study of age-friendly cities and communities has grossly overlooked the role of the church. To this we could also add the lack of attention to mosques, meeting houses, temples, synagogues and the buildings of many other organised religions.

So, the task of this section is to identify the role that religious organisations play as key parts of our neighbourhood social infrastructure. This is challenging because although there are undoubtedly significant spiritual benefits for those visiting a mosque or a church, we are less interested here in those benefits and are instead more concerned with the social benefits visiting these spaces might have. It is difficult to separate out these spiritual and emotional benefits from the social ones, but this section will attempt to do so by focusing as far as possible on what existing research says about the types of social interactions and connections that are developed in religious spaces and how these have been shown to support older people. What is also very difficult to separate are the benefits of 'being religious' or having a faith from actually visiting an FBO. Most of the existing literature appears to conflate the two, which is less helpful when trying to identify the importance of using a religious building as a site of social infrastructure versus having a faith and perhaps practising it in other ways.

This being said, some studies have looked more holistically at the wellbeing benefits brought to older people of being religious, and in some of these studies, it is possible to sift out how visiting a religious building provides opportunities for social interaction and connections. For example, Wink and Dillon (2003) identified the importance of social support and positive interpersonal relationships for older people attending church, and Fields et al. (2016) in their ethnically diverse study of older church goers in Texas, US, found that churches played an important role as a social connector, providing opportunities for volunteering and as a provider of health-related information. Interviews with older people in the latter study showed that attending church gave them the opportunity to develop social connections that would not otherwise have existed for them in the community, and volunteering with the church helped people feel more involved with community life and less socially isolated. Therefore, for the people who use them, churches and other FBOs are crucial parts of the social infrastructure of age-friendly communities.

The study of migrant churches makes a particularly helpful contribution to the study of social connections made through religious organisations. It also helps us consider the importance of this type of social infrastructure for different minority and migrant groups of older people. David Ley (2008) made a study of Chinese, Korean and German Christian churches in the Greater Vancouver area to explore the role these churches played in meeting the needs of its members as newcomers to Canada. The church members included in Ley's study were a mix of ages but tended to reflect immigration patterns to Canada and, therefore, represented an ageing population. What he found was that churches played a central role in providing a second home for migrants on arrival to the country. This was not just through a sense of spiritual and community belonging, although this was hugely valued, but it was also through the social networks created within the congregation. Ley found that individuals were able to amass a substantial amount of social capital and these networks of trust and reciprocity allowed for the sharing of advice, counselling and practical services between people.

There is little doubt that churches can help facilitate the type of bonding capital that is so important for helping migrants to settle in a new place. What is interesting from Ley's study is which identities new migrants bonded over in churches. Ley found that ethnicity, language, dialect and place of origin were much more important in bringing people together than religious values. In this instance, the churches acted as an umbrella organisation for migrants from a particular migration background rather than with religious values and practices in common. This also served to connect people across social boundaries. However, despite being an important place for the creation of strong bonding capital, Ley found that the migrant churches he studied were less successful in creating opportunities for bridging social capital. This then became a challenge when trying to bridge the generation gap between newer and more established migrants as well as supporting the integration of migrants into the wider community.

The wider role that religious organisations play in hosting community events means that FBO have an important part to play as social infrastructure for non-religious people. Therefore, the hosting of activities for community members outside of the congregation puts such FBOs in the position of being able to broker bridging social capital, bringing together people of different or no religion. However there are, of course, many people who would not feel either comfortable or welcomed in a religious setting, and, therefore, the potential for exclusion of certain groups is high.

From the review of literature presented here, it is clear that for many religious people, their faith organisations provide them with opportunities for building both strong and weak bonding capital, as they are coming together with others who share a common bond. Most of the existing research, however, tends to focus on Christian-based organisation. Whilst we might assume that similar social interactions occur within the religious buildings of Islamic or Jewish faiths, there will be important differences to consider such as the separation of men and women, for example, as this might affect the types of social interactions taking place. Therefore, much more research is needed into the social benefits of religious organisations for older people of non-Christian faiths.

Leisure Activities

Leisure pursuits provide a particular set of organised activities that can be crucial for both mental and physical well-being as we age and can be especially important for maintaining social connections. Leisure is a slightly different category when it comes to considering social infrastructures, however, as it is sometimes the activity itself, and not the space in which it takes place, which is the important focus when thinking about exactly how social interactions occur. Of course, some leisure activities will be tied to a particular building, such as group exercise in a sports centre, but some of the leisure pursuits can be considered as almost separate from their physical setting, for example, a local history group that meets in a pub, or a craft group meeting in a café or a walking group outdoors. In these instances, it would be how the organised group activity itself fosters social capital amongst its members that would be of interest, less so the space in which it takes place.

Having established that we need to keep in mind the difference between spaces of leisure and leisure activities themselves, we need to identify what we mean by leisure activities and which ones we will focus on in this section. Leisure activities can be defined as 'preferred and enjoyable activities participated in during free time' (Kleiber & Nimrod, 2009). As with any age group, older people are involved in a diversity of leisure activities; however, only a small subset of activities appears in social science studies. Some are directly related to physical health such as sports, whilst others may have a more indirect benefit on health and well-being such as participating in a nature and conservation group. Some leisure activities involve some degree of collective participation such as a craft group whilst others are more individual pursuits such as reading or gardening. Robert Putnam (2000) writes that it is the *doing* of activities together that is important for social connection, so this section will focus on a small selection of collective leisure activities and spaces that support the formation and maintenance of social capital. There are also many activities that fall under the definition of leisure that will not be discussed here because they are dealt with elsewhere in the book such as volunteering, shopping, and eating out and drinking.

Engaging in leisure pursuits has been found to have a myriad of physical and mental health benefits in later life, including reducing stress, enriching meaning of life and helping to overcome negative life events (Chang, Wray, & Lin, 2014). Existing studies of leisure in later life have taken a lifespan approach, looking at how experiences and events across the life course can influence leisure activities in later life. There is also a wealth of studies looking at the barriers to and benefit of engaging with certain leisure pursuits (Miller, 2016). 'Leisure serves as an indispensable vehicle for the formation, maintenance and sustainability of social ties' (Glover, 2018, p. 28), and although there is broad agreement in the literature that there is an association between taking part in certain leisure activities and acquiring social capital, there is some disagreement over the direction of this relationship. The majority of research focuses on how participation in leisure activities can actually make older people more sociable and more inclined to participate in other areas. Less research has focused on how different types of leisure pursuits help facilitate social connections for older people and what types of social connections these might be (Toepoel, 2013).

For the purposes of this discussion, we will focus on a select group of illustrative, but by no means exhaustive examples of leisure activities pursued in later life and consider how they might contribute to the social capital of individuals. Existing studies tend to cover a small range of leisure activities that are typically gendered in nature such as knitting, and craft groups aimed at women and men's shed type groups for older men. This may reflect the gendered nature of the types of social interventions aimed at older people, or it may just reflect the dominance of particular case studies within research. Some 'less' gendered examples do exist such as group exercise, community choirs and walking groups, so these have been included where possible but because of the diversity of leisure activities discussed it is difficult to draw any conclusions as to which types of activities are most helpful for supporting which types of social connections. Instead, this discussion will try to identify some commonalities across the different examples of collective organised leisure activities given.

Group exercise, whether it be team sports, a dance class or a walking group, has been shown to have significant physical and mental health benefits. Of most interest to the arguments of this book are the feelings of togetherness, collective belonging and community that these types of leisure pursuits can engender. Studies of group running events such as Parkrun (Wiltshire & Stevinson, 2018) and group exercise in gyms (Haslam et al., 2009; Markman, 2012) have demonstrated the sense of community that can be created and the social networks of support that develop from this. Specifically, with regard to older people, Joseph and Southcott's (2019) study of a line dancing class in Australia found that the friendships formed through this participation extended beyond the class to become important networks of care where people checked up on each other and were there to offer support and encouragement through different periods in their lives. Here we see the development of strong bonds of friendship, quite different from the weak ties of association developed though regularly visiting a local coffee shop, for example (discussed in the next chapter). Friendship was clearly a valued benefit of attending the group by the older people in this study. So too was meeting people from different walks of life. This is something that has been found by other studies of sports and fitness related leisure pursuits for older people. Hwang, Wang, Siever, Del Medico, and Jones (2019) study of a rehabilitative walking group in Canada has similar findings around an appreciation of diversity and a collective sense of belonging in the group (although there was no indication here of how this might translate into social connections between individuals), and studies of older people's involvement in organised sport has continually reported the interpersonal benefits to older people of being able to have intergenerational exchanges either informally through participation in sport, or more formally through mentoring and coaching (Jenkin, Eime, Westerbeek, O'Sullivan, & van Uffelen, 2016).

Craft-based groups, particularly around needlework, have seen something of a resurgence in recent years. As a social intervention into loneliness and isolation in later life, craft groups have become a firm favourite in both policy and research. Frequented in the majority by women, studies have found substantial benefits of friendship, support and skill sharing for older participants. One study of craft groups in Australia by Maidment and Macfarlane (2009) found that participants reported feeling less lonely and learning new skills as key benefits of this leisure activity. Their participants also talked about the importance of their craft group being a source of support outside of the family circle as it helped them maintain a sense of continuity and identity during difficult times of transition such as loss or illness. This has been qualified by other studies of involvement with handcraft guilds that have found involvement in such institutions 'can often be a conduit to healthy ageing, consciously chosen by women as a means of preserving autonomy and dealing effectively with life changing conditions' (Schofield-Thompson & Littrell, 2001, p. 50). This underlines Oldenburg and Bissetts' argument that third places, outside the family and the workplace, are essential for 'provid(ing) people with a larger measure of their sense of wholeness and distinctiveness' (Oldenburg & Bissett, 1982, p. 267). Many studies of craft-based groups have emphasised the importance of the friendships that develops out of these activities suggesting that organised activities such as this have a role to play as social infrastructure in facilitating the development of strong social capital. The composition of such groups, whether they bring together a diversity of people or have a narrower membership, will determine how far bridging capital will be facilitated. However, many other studies have pointed to the intergenerational aspect of knitting groups, for example, especially as knitting appears to be becoming more popular with younger generations and well as the potential for intercultural connections (Robinson, 2020).

Men's sheds have become a popular form of organised group activity aimed at older men in the United States, the United Kingdom and in Australia where the concept originated. They provide a communal space for older people to socialise and learn new skills. Activities usually focus on woodwork, and membership is usually exclusively men although not always. The rise in men's sheds can be attributed partly to a response to lower rates of men engaging in other types of organised community and social activity and higher rates of social isolation amongst some groups of older men. Therefore, groups such as men's sheds and other gendered social activities have been used as a way of addressing both these issues. In terms of their success, a scoping review of research into the impact on participants Milligan et al. (2016) concluded that such organised leisure groups did appear to have a positive impact on mental well-being and for participants and decreased loneliness. However, they caution that the existing data are limited, and there is a lack of longitudinal evidence of any effects. Although research into men's sheds has found participants benefit from feeling a sense of belonging through their involvement with the group, this does not tell us very much about the types of interactions that are had here, nor the types of social connections they produce and whether they exist outside of that setting.

Studies of participation in community choirs have been helpful in demonstrating a multiplier-type effect of involvement in organised leisure groups for older people. Langston's (2011) study of community choirs in Tasmania found that membership was a high predictor of engagement in other local community organisations. This has been attributed to a strong sense of belonging with organisations such as a choir which creates trust and practices of care between participants. Therefore, these social connections can be of benefit to both the individual and the wider community. It would appear then that participating in organised group leisure activities has the capacity at least to facilitate strong bonds between people who have a shared interest and have chosen to spend at least part of their leisure time pursuing it, but there is also the opportunity for these activities to bring together people of quite different backgrounds and thereby create social connections that act as bridges into other social worlds. The presumed regularity of engaging in these activities and the structure by which they are organised seem to lend themselves to developing strong bonds of friendship and support networks outside of the activity compared to less formalised activities such as visiting a coffee shop or individual visits to a local park, for example. We might assume that the more structured nature of the interactions might encourage more conversation of a deeper type which overtime can become the basis of friendships rather than acquaintanceships.

Despite there being a clear role for leisure in bringing people from different backgrounds together and the potential for the development of bridging capital as a result, Yuen and Johnson (2017) note that there is little serious engagement with the concept of third place within leisure studies. Leisure and recreation research have tended to focus on the meaning of leisure to the individual at the expense of its meaning to the community (Arai & Pedlar, 2003). This is an oversight as leisure has a clear role to play at the community level as well as that of the individual. However, we should be guarded against viewing organised leisure as a panacea for community and remain vigilant to the many ways in which leisure spaces can be exclusionary for some groups.

Many leisure studies point to the sense of belonging and togetherness fostered by collective leisure activity based on the development of trust, friendship and networks of support. They also point to a multiplier effect of participation meaning that once a person is involved in one group activity, they are likely to become involved in more. The concept of serious leisure, meaning activities which people do not make their living from but nonetheless constitute a central interest in their individual and collective lives (Stebbins, 1982), has been found by Heley and Jones (2013) to make a substantial and sustainable contribution to local communities. In their study in rural Wales, they found several examples of older people engaging in what the researchers defined as serious leisure that had positive impacts for the rest of the community. Examples included individuals taking their passion for local history and setting up a local history walking group or the local Anglers groups setting up an armature competition to encourage younger residents to become more involved in the natural habitat of the area. This is excellent news for both community cohesion and community development as it shows the social connections developed in a community choir, for example, can potentially have a ripple effect far beyond the individual and can help support a vibrant and active community and voluntary sector locally.

PUBLIC SERVICES AND INSTITUTIONS

For the purpose of this book, a discussion of public services and institutions as social infrastructure will focus on the examples of public libraries, schools and other educational institutions. Although these shared spaces do host organised activities (like the examples discussed above), it is not their main function and being, for the most part, services that are provided by the state, they occupy a rather different position within the community than the types of organised social activities as identified by Jeffres et al. (2009). A selective review of the literature around older people and transportation is also included in this section in recognition of the importance of public services that enable older people to access other forms of social infrastructure.

Schools and other Educational Institutions

For Eric Klinenberg (2018), educational institutions are essential parts of social infrastructure especially in neighbourhoods low in other resources. However, the roles of schools and other educational institutions remain, for the most part, an under-utilised resource in many communities. Within age-friendly communities, the role of schools is most commonly discussed in relation to their role in hosting intergenerational programmes. These are organised programmes of work, sometimes led by the school itself but also commonly ran in collaboration with the local state and sometimes third-sector organisations. A more detailed discussion of intergenerational community relationships is developed in Chapter 6, however, to briefly summarise here the majority of research on intergenerational relationships outside of the family tend to focus on those connections that have been developed as a result of targeted and intentional intergenerational programmes and events. There is much less research on the type of intergenerational connections that might occur organically as a result of people of different ages simply using a shared space together. Therefore, when it comes to examining the role of schools as social infrastructure, and specifically how they might benefit the social connectedness of older people, most of the evidence comes from the evaluation of purposeful intergenerational programmes based in schools and not how schools might facilitate the *informal* mixing of younger and older people.

Long established examples of the intergenerational potential of schools can be seen in Sweden's 'Classroom Grandads' and Japans Gakusha Yugo projects (translated to unity of schools and community) both of which embed a commitment to lifelong learning within in the curriculum. The most common form of intergenerational programme in schools' is older volunteers assisting with classroom activities or specially designed intergenerational projects such as gardening and storytelling projects. Evaluation of such programmes are limited, but benefits to older people are commonly found to be feeling more valued in their communities, gaining in confidence and skills and higher self-esteem (Raynes & Rawlings, 2004; Stanton, 2003). Wider community level benefits include greater community cohesion and integration between generations although there is limited information as to how this is measured and how sustainable these effects are.

Klinenberg argues that schools, colleges and universities can play significant roles as social infrastructure in their communities depending on how they are designed, managed and on the programmes they run. Despite there being little research evidence that explicitly focuses on how schools might function as third places, there are studies that have focused on other third places that we can draw upon in thinking about how schools can operate as important social infrastructure for older people. Studies of community groups and third-sector organisations that are focused on children, for example, have often highlighted the indirect social benefits these spaces bring to the parents of their younger patrons. Jupp (2013), for example, demonstrated the importance informal support networks that developed between mothers attending children's centres in England. In this instance, the 'homeliness' of the children's centres provided a sense of comfort and security for the parents and created an atmosphere where they felt they could speak openly and seek help if they needed it.

Klinenberg (2018) discusses the example of a school in Manhattan where parents of very young children are encouraged to join them in the classroom for the first 15 minutes of the day. This was presented as a way for the child to become acclimatised to the new school environment but in actual fact served as an informal way for the parents to meet and get to know one another. Not able to carry on conversations inside the school building once the initial 15 minutes was up, a relatively large open space, equipped with benches and small trees, immediately outside the main school doors provided a relaxed space for parents to linger and chat. Nearby coffee shops provide a venue for these conversations and relationships to develop further. Klinenberg contrasts this laid back and fluid management of school drop-offs with the altogether more regimented and efficient systems of drop-offs from vehicles at the school gates that occurs in many other schools. Schools that do not have the adequate space to allow social interaction at the school gates are therefore, Klinenberg argues, at a disadvantage in being able to create a sense of community amongst parents.

However, the ability to support these types of social interactions can also be down to management and programming. Klinenberg discusses how even large schools with big intakes can be designed to create smaller learning communities that allow students and teachers to become closer, and for parents to develop local knowledge and feel a higher level of personal and emotional investment in the school. He suggests too that this can allow community trust and familiarity to develop from becoming familiar with the same teachers, students and families year on year. Research such as this demonstrates the potential of schools to act as important social infrastructures for older people especially when we consider the increased childcare roles grandparents take on which, in many cases, will involve dropping off and collecting children from school. Depending on how the school operates, this will expose the older people concerned to wider social networks.

Klinenberg makes a useful discussion of the similar ways in which university campus have, in recent years, been experimenting with new forms of civic engagement with the wider communities in which they are located and to move away from outdated 'town and gown' divisions. These approaches extend beyond the corporate social responsibility agenda and towards co-produced research, providing space for community events, public lectures and workshops and local job creation. This presents important opportunities for older adults living in the community to become involved in such institutions, to improve their connections in the community and make their own social connections. However, any such programming must have an equalities approach at its heart in order to avoid replicating existing inequalities.

Public Libraries

Committed to a principle of openness (Muddiman et al., 2001), public libraries have the potential to draw in a diversity of users from across the community making them particularly important as a space of social infrastructure. Klinenberg (2018) describes public libraries as one of the most important, yet undervalued examples of social infrastructure in Western societies. They provide a free, safe and inclusive space often acting as a place of refuge for those social groups who may experience social exclusion such as some younger people, some older adults as well as those who are homeless.

They have both a socialisation role and a role in supporting meaningful encounters with difference. As Klinenberg notes:

> *After all, places like libraries are saturated with strangers, people whose bodies are different, who make different sounds, speak different languages, give off different, sometimes noxious smells. Spending time in public social infrastructure requires learning to deal with these differences in a civil manner.*
>
> *(Klinenberg, 2018, p. 45)*

Libraries allow an ambivalent space for people of different backgrounds to be around each other but also to learn from the subtle cues of each other's behaviour in a way where no one group is the 'host'. Different social groups pass by one another and are able to interact with each other in a unidirectional, non-orchestrated way.

Despite their importance as spaces of social life, very little sociological research exists on what occurs in libraries themselves (Vårheim, 2009). In terms of who actually visits public libraries, we can glean some information from membership data that suggest older people are more likely than younger people to be members of a library (Linley, 2011), but this does not mean they visit the library more often. Data from a UK Government sponsored survey, *Taking Part* in 2018, found that there is higher library use in England amongst black and Asian ethnic groups compared to white ethnic groups. But again, this only tells us a partial story. Overall, studies of public libraries agree they attract a broad spectrum of users, being free to use and open to all. The fifth of S.R.Ranganathan's *The Five Laws of Library Service* (1931) states that 'the library is a growing organism' meaning that it should continually evolve to meet the needs of its users. This very much situates the public library as an important part of social infrastructure serving its local neighbourhood.

Little is known about the types of interactions that occur within a library, but we can infer a certain amount by thinking about how they are used and by whom. Klinenberg praises the programmed events and activities of libraries in particular, for providing the opportunity for social contact for potentially lonely and isolated people within a community. However, it is also the more informal use of libraries, outside of curated activities, that are just as important for social interactions. Working from the assumption that public libraries will draw in a diversity of different social, cultural and age groups from across the local community, it would seem safe to assume that there is great potential for libraries to function as passing places and to facilitate the type of everyday conviviality with difference that is so essential to living in diverse, particularly in urban, settings.

Robinson (2020) has considered this in relation to everyday multicultur-alism in her ethnographic study of a knitting group that met in a public library in South London. The all-female group was made up of middle aged to older women from a diversity of ethnic backgrounds reflecting the wider local population. From analysing the interactions of the group members, and informally interviewing the women themselves, Robinson concluded that informal groups using public libraries, such as the knitting group, have the capacity to act as sites of everyday multiculturalism. In the interactions between the women in this group, Robinson identified moments of 'hopeful gestures' (Wise, 2005) of reciprocity and mutual recognition between the ethnically different individuals. However, Robison is cautious not to overstate the positivity of these types of interactions. They are neither inevitable nor inconsequential she argues and cites Neal, Bennett, Jones, Cochrane, and Mohan (2015) in reminding us that 'power and histories of racism are as much a part of the everyday picture as convivialities and affinities'. Just as much as there is the potential for meaningful encounters with difference in public libraries, there is equally the potential for discrimination and prejudice. However, based on the principle of openness that public libraries represent, they can offer a space of understated connection and care therefore forming a vital part of our social infrastructure.

Public Transport

One of Oldenburg's (1989) core principles of third places was that they should be local in the sense that residents are able to access them on foot. He felt that if one had to drive or take public transport to reach somewhere then casual, drop-in nature of that venue would be lost. Having good quality social infrastructure within walkable distance is certainly a key element of age-friendly neighbourhoods, and research continues to show the importance of local amenities to well-being. Reporting on data from the American Enterprise Institute Survey on Community and Society, Cox and Streeter (2019) point to an 'amenities effect' to explore this. Defined expansively in this survey as spaces such as parks, libraries, restaurants and shops, Cox and Streeter concluded that living in an area with a high concentration of amenities can increase our sense of satisfaction with our neighbourhood, make us more likely to remain living there, make us more likely to trust and lend a hand to our neighbours, make us take more of an interest in local events and decrease the chance of experiencing social isolation or feeling lonely. However, social infrastructure that is accessible on foot is not possible in all neighbourhoods nor is it an option for all residents. Older people living with some form of physical impairment or mobility issue often rely on transportation to be able to lead independent lives. Therefore, in considering the social infrastructure needs of age-friendly neighbourhoods, we must also think about how different forms of transportation (from private cars to community and public transport) facilitate older people's access to opportunities for social encounter.

The social needs of older people are part of Musselwhite and Haddad's (2010) three-tier model developed to explain older people's motivation for travel and mobility. The primary need identified by his model is a utilitarian one; mobility that meets a practical need to travel from one place to another. Sometimes this can be to meet social needs such as travelling to a park or café to meet friends and be around others, but these needs can also be about attending medical appointments and doing grocery shopping. The secondary mobility motivation identified by Musselwhite and Haddad are psychosocial needs; the need for independence and preservation of identity and sense of self and the third was an aesthetic motivation to be able to visit somewhere 'simply to see, sense, feel or experience mobility or travel itself and to be mobile for its own sake' (2010, p. 50). This model is useful when thinking about the social infrastructure needs of age-friendly communities as it draws attention to the more affective and emotional needs for mobility in later life as well as the functional needs.

Researchers have also looked into the different forms of transportation older people use and their various benefits. Some forms of transportation have more social benefits than others which are important when considering transportation as social infrastructure as well as providing access to other shared spaces. Musselwhite and Haddad (2018) found that it was access to and use of a private car that was often the most valued by older people in helping them meet the three different levels of mobility needs. Whilst being able to drive oneself offered maximum independence and mobility for many, car ownership and the ability to drive are not available to all older people. In the United Kingdom, 40% of households do not have access to the use of a car, and low-income neighbourhoods and households occupied by older people are heavily concentrated in this group (Lucas, Stokes, Bastiaanssen, & Burkinshaw, 2019). Therefore, many older people either come to rely upon some other form of transportation in later life, or in many cases, have always had to travel by other means. Receiving lifts from friends, family members or neighbours was often viewed as a satisfactory alternative to being able to drive one's own car. Musselwhite and Haddad (2018) found that receiving lifts allowed older people to maintain their social engagements and, therefore, remain connected to their social networks. It also facilitated connections between the older person and those driving them, especially in the case of neighbours and family members. Older people often commented on appreci-ating being able to spend time with younger relatives during journeys.

Outside of private forms of transport, public and community transport often form central aspects of age-friendly neighbourhoods in providing ways in which older people can both maintain some degree of independence as well as meet their social and everyday needs.

Public transport has been found to be hugely important to many older people in allowing them to be able to access other important social infra-structures and maintain and build social connections and reduce social isola-tion (Doran & Buffel, 2018). As older people tend to spend more of their time in their immediate neighbourhoods, policy around age-friendly transport can often focus more on meeting these utilitarian and practical needs to ensure older people can access local facilities. Although this is important, it is often at odds with transport policy more generally which prioritises hypermobility and movement across larger areas (Parkhurst et al., 2014). An example of the implications of this comes from a co-produced research project on age-friendly neighbourhoods in Greater Manchester in the United Kingdom (Doran & Buffel, 2018), where cuts to particular bus routes had become a cause for concern in relation to increased social isolation of older residents. Through the co-research approach of this project, those involved were able to persuade local policymakers of the importance of this particular bus route and to get it re-instated.

Further research evidence suggesting the need to take a wider perspective in age-friendly transport policy comes from studies of older people from partic-ular minority ethnic communities which find older people often using public transport to travel significant distances outside of their local area to visit important spaces of social infrastructure such as parks and specialist food markets and retailers. Yarker's (2020) research found that such spaces were not only important in practical terms, such as being able to access culturally specific food products but that they were also important ways of older people maintaining social networks with people who shared the same cultural, ethnic or religious background to themselves.

Community transport, the provision of off time-table services usually aimed at a specific population who typically cannot access mainstream public transport, has also been found to be hugely important to those older people who use it. As well as providing a low-cost method of travelling, community transport has also been found to be an important social infrastructure in itself by creating a space for social connections and a sense of belonging to develop (Musselwhite, 2017). However, Musselwhite (2017) also found that community transport suffered something of an image problem amongst those older people who did not use it. Comments from participants in this research suggested that community transport was seen as residual and for those who had few other options. This is problematic as further research from Musselwhite suggests that it was the social aspect of community transport in particular that was of most value to those who used it.

Existing research on older people's use of different methods of transportation shows that transport is important for the social connections of older people through both providing a means by which to access other forms of social infrastructure, as well as being a part of age-friendly social infrastructure in itself. Public and community transport in particular can provide spaces of casual and passing interactions and the potential over time for developing weak social ties. All forms of transport are able to open up the social worlds of older people by giving them access to meeting with friends and family members. Therefore, it is important that we consider age-friendly transport as social infrastructure in itself and to ensure neighbourhoods are well linked with other places as well as within the locality.

A SPACE IN WHICH TO BRING PEOPLE TOGETHER

The types of social interaction that occur within organised activities were the main focus of Robert Putnam's widely cited intervention into the social capital literature. They provide regular, structured interactions between a group, or groups, of people coming together for a common purpose and with some shared form of identity, background, experience or interests. As social infrastructures then, organised activities are very good at creating bonding capital and also strong ties of friendship and support. Putnam lamented the decline in participation in these types of organised group activities; however, it appears this may have been an oversimplification of the situation, and participation in organised activities continues to be popular amongst all ages, despite changes in how we use our leisure time and engage with others. However, more than any other type of infrastructure, there is the potential for certain organised group activities to be exclusionary; therefore, organisations need to ensure they work with an equalities mindset to overcome barriers and forms of discrimination that may exclude certain groups. This means looking beyond statutory categories of discrimination or protected characteristics and instead placing those people and groups who may be at the margins of communities, at the centre of organised activity development and design (Ambition for Ageing, 2019).

Religious organisations and the community and voluntary sector in particular provide a wealth of opportunities for social interaction for older people. However, for many, structural, emotional and cultural barriers still exist in accessing these types of social infrastructures. Therefore, as well as working to reduce these barriers, we must also become more aware of the social potential of our public services. Both through their programming of community facing events, as well as through the public service they provide, institutions such as schools and libraries are vital in bringing community members together with the opportunity of having meaningful encounters with those who are different from themselves.

5

COMMERCIAL VENUES

Commercial venues are of particular interest as social infrastructure, as although the primary remit might not be a social one, they are a vital and regular part of the everyday lives of many older people and therefore become important sites of social interaction. The list of venues that could be included in this section is vast. For the purpose of this discussion, we will separate 'Retail and Commercial Services' from hospitality spaces of 'Eating, drinking and talking', the latter following on from the loose adoption of Jeffres, Bracken, Jian, and Casey (2009) classification of third places. For our purposes a discussion of commercial enterprise will include spaces that concern shopping and service provision; therefore, this section will consider the role of high streets, markets, commercial services, such as banks and post offices, and personal services, such as beauty salons and barbershops. This list is not exhaustive by any means but it does reflect some of the commercial spaces that are the most prominent in research on older people's use of commercial venues.

RETAIL AND COMMERCIAL SERVICES

The category of retail and commercial services is expansive. It includes all types of shops, retail outlets, markets and any service-based enterprises from banks, hairdressers to mobile phone repair shops, bookmakers and tattoo parlours. It is, therefore, impossible to cover all types of retail space in this discussion, and indeed there is little, if any, research explicitly focusing on some of these spaces. Therefore, the decision was made to focus on research on markets and various commercial services as these are retail sites which have a more obvious social function, especially for older people, and for which there was some research evidence for.

Markets

Markets have been described as one of the most crucial yet neglected spaces in our local communities (Watson & Studdert, 2006). In 2009, the Retail Markets Alliance reported that an estimated 96,000 people in Britain were directly employed by markets and that they boasted an annual turnover of £7.6 billion (Gonzalez & Waley, 2012). In addition to their economic contributions, markets also contribute to the social life and cultural diversity of a place. Despite this the picture of markets in the United Kingdom is one of mixed fortunes. Many traditional markets, with their diverse mix of local and independent traders, have been in decline in recent years, due to lack of investment, competition from other retail offerings, changes in consumer tastes and poor management (Gonzalez & Waley, 2012). However, due to an increasing awareness of the potential for markets to act as a catalyst for local economic development, many have been the subject of redevelopment leading Gonzalez and Waley to describe markets as the 'new frontier of gentrification' (2012). The recently identified position of markets as vehicles of local economic development has seen a growth in niche or specialist markets such as Christmas Markets, Farmers Markets and specialist food markets. These changes in the role and position of local markets, whether they are in decline, have been redeveloped or the emergence of new types of markets will both reflect and amplify the changing economic fortunes and the social and cultural lives of the communities around them.

Traditional markets can be spaces of cultural vibrancy and diversity, often in direct comparison to the seemingly more homogenous space of shopping malls. With their culturally diverse offerings and lower price points, markets have historically been popular with both newly arrived migrants and more established migrant communities. As a result, research on markets has often identified them as key sites of everyday multiculturalism, where people from different cultural, ethnic and religious backgrounds can come into regular contact with one another. We can therefore think of markets as important passing places with the potential for bringing together diverse groups of people, for facilitating the mixing of these groups and for the development of bridging ties.

Markets have always functioned as social levellers (Morales, 2009). Empirical research by Rivlin and González (2018) into Leeds Kirkgate Market in the United Kingdom found high levels of 'recognition, adaptation and civility across multiple difference' (p. 4, drawing on Anderson, 2011). These were 'spontaneous acts of sociability' typically manifesting themselves as nods, smiles and waves between individuals. There were also examples of everyday negotiations around language such as interactions between customers and traders using notepads and mobile phones for translation and traders adapting their retailer offerings to meet different cultural needs. The low barrier of entry to markets, their typically low cost of goods and produce, coupled with an informal atmosphere means markets can often provide spaces where boundaries between different groups can momentarily disappear (Mele, Ng, & Bo Chim, 2015). As such, they have been found to bring about what Watson and Gonsalez identified as 'elective affinities' often framed in relation to social class. For example, in their interviews, one British Asian trader stated that regardless of the cultural background of customers, everyone was working class in the market. However, despite there being potential for meaningful contact with difference within markets, it is important to recognise that social interactions in markets can just as easily reinforce difference as well as they can transcend it (Amin, 2002). Therefore, it is important not to overstate the cohesive potential of these interactions on their own and to remember that civility is not the same as acceptance. As Noble (2011) reminds us, people may act in both cosmopolitan and racist ways at different moments.

These cautions withstanding, both the informality and diversity of markets do at least open up the possibility of inclusion for those social groups which may be the most marginalised such as those on low incomes, newly arrived migrants and older people. Indeed, much of the research into the sociality of markets points to their importance as social spaces for older shoppers. There are a number of elements which contribute to this. Firstly, many traditional markets have long histories in a community meaning that for many older people they act as important markers in their biographies with connections to childhood, family and a sense of insiderness to place (Rowles, 1983). Secondly, the sometimes quieter, slower pace and more familiar setting of a market can often be preferable to some older people as they offer the opportunity for relaxed social interactions as well as a retail experience. The provision of low-cost cafes has been found to be crucial in furthering this appeal (Watson & Studdert, 2006) and finally, market traders have been found to play a central role in increasingly the age-friendliness of markets.

Traders have regular interactions with their older customers, often on a weekly or sometimes daily basis. They become familiar strangers with each other through the development of weak ties of association that can become important networks of social support. Research on this topic is full of anecdotes of traders helping older customers back to their cars with shopping, looking after shopping for them while they walk around the market, providing informal seating areas, hot drinks and pleasant conversation. When needed, traders have also been known to check up on customers who may have been unwell or suffered a bereavement and to pass information on to others about their well-being. In short, traders play a central role in not only making the market a welcoming place for older people to visit but also in providing the conditions for further social interactions and networks of support to develop. As described, these networks tend to be based in weak ties of acquaintance, where faces are recognised but full names might not be known. However, this level of informality itself goes some way in providing conditions in which older people can socialise without obligation and develop, nonetheless, important connections without any expectation.

Research into the use of markets by older people from particular minority ethnic groups has also found that being able to interact with other customers and traders who share a similar cultural identity to themselves is particularly important for maintaining a sense of cultural identity in later life. Older women from the South Asian community in particular reported certain markets as being an important space for socialising and to visit with friends demonstrating the importance of these spaces for facilitating strong bonding capital (Yarker, 2020). However, just as important was the fleeting interactions with other customers and traders to catch up with and discuss news from their home countries as well as share personal updates about family. Therefore, it was also the opportunity to engage in passing and less formal interactions and to develop weak social ties that were valued in visiting a market. This sociability was felt to be just as important as being able to access culturally specific products, and many older people in this study were prepared to travel quite some distance from their home to visit these places.

Having established the importance of markets as social infrastructure, what then are the different features of markets that support them to function as social spaces? Firstly, they need to provide opportunities to linger; therefore, they need to operate with the opposite mindset of efficiency where people might move through a space quickly and purposefully. Instead, markets need to capitalise on their more informal nature and their flexibility to ensure people can take their time as they move through the space and have opportunities to stop, sit, chat or simply people-watch without feeling the pressure to move on or to make a purchase. Here, markets can offer a more relaxed and informal retail experience, with the potential for individuals to appropriate the space with greater freedom and agency compared to the rather more controlled environment of a shopping mall, which tends to have an altogether more sanitised environment and greater formal (as well as informal) surveillance.

In addition to the general laid-back atmosphere of a market, there are practical things that can help facilitate lingering and therefore social interaction. The provision of seating, especially for older customers, has been seen time and time again in research on age-friendly communities to be central in encouraging older people to feel confident in using a space and for engaging in social interactions once they are there. Toilet facilities are also crucial in supporting older people to be able to visit public spaces such as markets. Research by Watson and Studdert (2006) found that markets with the most vibrant social life were those with cafes, which again encouraged people to stay longer in the space and to interact with others. In addition, markets need to be well laid out, connect with other retail outlets in the area, have efficient management and good access and support an active and engaged community of traders and stallholders (Watson & Studdert, 2006).

Commercial and Personal Services

Commercial and personal services such as post offices, hair salons and banks are the everyday and often overlooked elements of our high streets, yet the offerings on our high streets can often be a good indication of the fortunes of local economies. Process of urban regeneration and gentrification can lead to new services and amenities geared towards particular age demographics with certain levels of expendable income and cultural tastes. Urban decline or a fall in household incomes of local residents can lead to the closure of shops and services, a growth in discount retailers and charity shops and a higher presence of shop voids. Another significant disappearance from the local high street in the United Kingdom is the presence of high-street services such as bank branches and post offices. Due to pressures to cut costs, banks will often look to close local branches or relocate them elsewhere, with the total number of bank and building society branches in the United Kingdom falling by 28% between 2012 and 2020 (Booth, 2021). There is evidence to suggest that it is high streets in the more economically disadvantaged neighbourhoods that bear the brunt of these closures (*The Guardian*, 22 July 2019) and it is typically older members of these neighbourhoods who suffer the most as a result. This can lead to the increased financial exclusion of some of the most vulnerable members of our communities who rely on local amenities the most. Research has found that those aged over 50 are the most likely to rely on local branches for accessing their money and would be most likely to switch their banks to one that did offer a local branch if their current one was to close. Research from Age UK has also stressed the importance of face-to-face banking for older people in preventing them from becoming the victim in financial scams and in combating social isolation (2016). Therefore, this underlines the importance of having amenities such as banks within walking distance for older residents and their importance as social infrastructures.

A similar picture can be found when looking at the impacts of post office closures in the United Kingdom. A survey carried out by UK Citizens Advice (2017) found that 65% of those aged 65 years and older saw the post office as very or extremely important to them, ranking it as the second most important community facility after banks, pubs or community centres. This is partly because older people often rely on post offices for their personal banking but also because it acted as a key passing place in the community where they would bump into friends and people they knew. People living with disabilities and on low incomes of all ages were also found to be the most frequent users of their local post office branch, with 15% of those surveyed by Citizens Advice saying they would lose contact with neighbours and friends if their local branch was to close, with those over 65 being the group most likely to state they would be affected. Therefore, for the most vulnerable members in our communities, including older people, those on low incomes and those with disabilities, post offices can be seen to provide an important service as well as social function and can therefore be considered vital parts of our social infrastructure.

Throughout this book we have seen the importance of everyday spaces as social infrastructures. Most of us visit these unassuming places with some degree of regularity. Personal care services, such as hairdressers, beauty salons and barbershops, provide an example of spaces that we might visit for other purposes, but that can become an important space for social interaction and the development of social connections. There is little research evidence that explicitly focuses on these spaces as sites of social interaction; however, looking to research on health promotion, we find a small, yet growing body of research into the importance of these types of spaces for community health intervention work for these very reasons.

Barbershops and beauty and hair salons are located in most communities and visited by a diversity of people on a regular basis and therefore can be helpful when trying to reach populations who may not engage with statutory services or community organisations (Linnon, D'Angelo, Cherise, & Harrington, 2014). In evaluations of health promotion work in these spaces, they have been found to be successful in actioning health behaviour change and increasing knowledge around certain health conditions. Some studies have concluded that this success is down to barbershops and beauty salons representing 'safe' spaces that also have a social dimension to them. The unique and trusting relationships customers develop with staff in these places were also found to be particularly important. With the presence of a social atmosphere, their unassuming and everyday nature and their regularity of use, it can be reasonably assumed that what makes barbershops and beauty salons useful in community health intervention work will also make them important spaces of social infrastructure. Again, this might be particularly relevant to older people who spend more time in their communities and who may experience social exclusion from other commercial spaces.

The relationship between staff and customers is a unique feature of social infrastructures that also have a commercial remit and this will be explored further in the next section on hospitality spaces. However, what becomes apparent from the above discussion of commercial enterprises is that there are social consequences, as well as economic ones, for a neighbourhood when these sites are under threat. A declining market in a town centre, for example, threatens the viability of other retail outlets around it, and a declining footfall means a decline in opportunities for social interaction. And whilst post offices and banks might not be the most glamorous features of our local high streets, the social interactions they facilitate can help contribute to community cohesion and help reduce isolation for some of the most vulnerable in our communities.

EATING, DRINKING AND TALKING

Establishments that make up the hospitality sector, places such as cafes, pubs, bars and restaurants, can provide a space of informal, non-obligatory social connections for older people as well as a destination for socialising with friends and family. Existing research on the social use of hospitality spaces by older people tends to be case study-orientated, for example, researching the use of a specific coffee shop or pub so this section will pull a collection of those studies together to see what we can learn from their collective analysis about the role these spaces play as social infrastructures for older people.

Cafes, Coffee Shops and Restaurants

In reviewing existing research on older people's use of cafes, coffee shops and restaurants, a striking theme in the research is a disagreement on the virtues, or otherwise, of independent establishments versus corporate chains. In the past, chain restaurants, along with other hospitality establishments, have been accused of being non-places due to their standardised, globalised and decontextualised nature (Augé, 1995). Perhaps most famously Ritzer (2006, 2008) has used the concept of McDonaldisation to draw attention to the emphasis on standardisation, predictability and control in these establishments, which might instinctively feel at odds with the kind of playful pure sociability described by Simmel (1949) as crucial in making a space a third place. Indeed, much of the critical social science literature around urban development and community laments the loss of independent shops and cafes as the result of urban regeneration. When privately, and often locally, owned businesses are forced to close due to rent increases, gentrification or loss of their core market, accusations of social exclusion are often rightly levelled at the chain operations that take their place. Local customers can be excluded by price but also culturally as the more affluent tastes and symbolic capital of chain coffee shops, for example, may not reflect the tastes and cultures of the existing community. However, whilst the instinct within critical social science might be to regret the presence of more generic and chain-owned hospitality outlets in our neighbourhoods, there is evidence within the literature to suggest that they can have a positive role to play as social infrastructure for older people.

For example, a study of second-generation Japanese American older people living in Honolulu by Cheang (2002) found that it was precisely the relaxed and informal setting of the local branch of a national fast-food restaurant chain that drew older people there to meet and socialise on a regular basis. During interviews with the 'regulars', the researchers found that it was a combination of the physical accessibility of the place, the free coffee refills on offer and the friendly and welcoming staff that contributed to the relaxed atmosphere. These older people chose to meet there on an informal basis because they did not feel they needed either the support or the structure of more formal groups and organisations aimed specifically at older people; 'senior centres are for old folks', one of their participants commented. Meeting in a fast-food outlet, however, gave them a sense of freedom and control over the space to come and go as they pleased and to use how best benefited them. The study went on to analyse the types of social interaction that the neutral environment of the fast-food chain supported for these older patrons. What they found was a certain type of casual sociability taking place characterised by play, fun and laughter. Conversation tended to be kept light, general and inconsequential and very little was discussed of a personal or sensitive nature. This is reminiscent of Simmel's concept of pure sociability where 'interaction existed for its own sake (and became) spoiled if its contents grows significant or its emotional impacts too strong' (1949, p. 163).

The impact of this type of sociability was that the relationships that developed between these patrons were context-specific and ceased to exist outside of that setting. Members of the group would ask after someone's ill husband, for example, but not visit them at home or at the hospital. Nonetheless, these relationships were important. A sense of community was created amongst this group of older people as well as a feeling of belonging which was underlined further by the practice of eating together – something which can be incredibly important for older people who live on their own. These types of social connections demonstrate the strength of weak ties as discussed by Granovetter. They were not strong social connections but they were, nonetheless, meaningful and important.

However, it is not just the verbal interactions that occur in hospitality spaces that are important. Jones et al. (2015) draw on Goffman's concept of civil inattention (1963) to show how even non-verbal co-presence in a third place such as a coffee shop or fast-food chain can be evidence of a slow burning multiculturalism made possible by the anonymity of chain hospitality spaces. For Goffman, civil inattention meant being around difference but not being fearful of it, hostile towards it or wishing to avoid it. Therefore, the types of interactions identified in some hospitality spaces could be seen as the types of delicate interaction and slight sociality that make up how we negotiate difference in our everyday lives and in everyday spaces.

A review of literature on third places by Rosenbaum (2006) supports these findings arguing that for those individuals who have recently lost their usual support networks, through relocating or retirement, for example, commercial spaces can be essential in sustaining supportive relationships. The review draws on the concept of 'commercial friendships' from Stones' (1954) study of women in the 1950s who had moved to a new city following their husbands' career. The relationships with both staff and other customers in frequently visited commercial settings served as a surrogate for the support networks these women had left behind. At some stage in later life, we tend to lose some or all of our usual support networks either through the death or illness of a spouse, retiring from the workforce or moving home. Therefore, we can start to see how the concept of 'commercial friendships' made in the context of a loss of support could be relevant to ageing. Unlike Cheang's study, however, Rosenbaum, Ward, Walker, and Ostrom (2007) found that these relationships were capable of extending outside of the commercial setting and that rich sources of support developed from these weak ties. Rosenbaum concludes his paper with some observations on what makes a hospitality venue a good third place. He argues they should be somewhere that people feel they can linger and with comfortable seating to encourage socialising – all elements identified above.

It can often be the neutral, and sometimes 'blandscape', nature of chain environments that can enable regular customers to feel at ease in a space. Based on their observational research of three chain restaurants and coffee shops in the United Kingdom, Jones et al. (2015) found that café regulars provided a sense of continuity for other customers and that it is these recognitions and exchanges that meant the corporate nature of the space became blended with small-scale localism. Therefore, the branch of the chain restaurant became *of* the place in which they were located and not separate from it. This is an important aspect in social infrastructure becoming a third place through the use of its patrons, the sociality generated within it and the meanings ascribed to it.

Therefore, it is not about pitting chain coffee shops against independent ones and arguing which one is best as functioning as a third place. Hopefully, the discussion here has demonstrated that it is down to the micro-geographies at work in each space as to how patrons will appropriate it and make it their own. However, what would be a mistake would be to underestimate the role that chain establishments can play on our high streets and in our communities. They should not, as Jones et al. argue, 'be dismissed as commercial, globalised spaces of soulless homogeneity', but can be 'locally inflected spaces whose cultural blandness may generate confident familiarity … and mundane co-presence' (p. 644). These establishments have a role to play as part of a diverse ecosystem of social infrastructure as they can mean different things to different people. Regular patrons of these establishments imbue them with their own social and cultural meanings and the neutrality and corporate nature of these environments can often facilitate this place making rather than undermine it.

An emerging point of interest around the use of hospitality venues is their potential role for engaging men in age-friendly programmes. Evidence on the social participation of older people in organised community-based activities shows a clear dominance of middle-class women (Milligan et al., 2016). Men from working class or from minority ethnic backgrounds, typically, tend to be less involved in formal activities such as volunteering and have lower rates of memberships in community associations and organisations. The exception to this is organisations based around sports. Therefore, when age-friendly work, aimed at increasing social connections for older people, starts from a community and voluntary organisation, there is often an initial difficulty in engaging men from lower socioeconomic or minority ethnic backgrounds. One age-friendly project in Camden, UK, decided to take this matter into their own hands and used outreach work as a way of engaging with working-class men living in their area. From this they found that the best places to find these men were precisely the types of mundane and everyday hospitality venues we have been discussing above (Mainey, 2019). This supports previous studies that it was the neutrality of these spaces, not associated with any common interest or any expected activity, that offered some men an easy and obligation free way of socialising (Broughton, Payne, & Liechty, 2017).

Pubs

The local pub provides an interesting dimension to a discussion on hospitality as social infrastructure. In the UK context in particular, the local pub has occupied a central role in the fabric of British society for many years (Jennings, 2007). Studies from the Mass Observation Archive (1943) point to the important role played by pubs in encouraging and enhancing social connectivity and community belonging, and more recently, the research from the Campaign for Real Ale (CAMRA) has noted the continued role of pubs as community hubs. This is despite a challenge to their status through trends towards drinking at home and the availability of cheap alcohol in supermarkets. Social science research continues to find that pubs remain at the heart of their communities with benefits both to the individuals who use them and to the wider community they are a part of (Cabras & Mount, 2017).

Pubs are far from homogenous. There is great diversity between them and with that comes a diversity in how they function as social infrastructure and the types of social interactions they produce. Thurnell-Read (2020) carried out a study into how older adults used pubs as part of their socialising in various different geographical and socioeconomic contexts in England. He found different groups of older people using pubs for different reasons and having different types of social interactions as a result. Amongst his participants, he noted a subgroup of older men who he referred to as 'regulars'. These were men who visited a preferred pub maybe once or twice a week; they usually visited alone and typically consumed one or two drinks. Their visits formed part of their typical everyday lives, usually whilst running errands and whilst there they might engage in small talk with the staff or other customers. This was especially important for those men who lived on their own. The role of staff was often crucial here in making these men feel welcome and valued. Thurnell-Read reported staff members talking of the importance of learning customers' first names, choice of drink and sometimes some other small detail about their lives such as their sporting preference. This underlines the importance of a 'host' or hosting type role in maintaining the social element of social infrastructure. Based on interviews with these individuals and pub staff, these visits, although fleeting and informal, were often crucial for the individual to feel part of the community and for having some form of social interaction with others.

However, this study did find evidence of older people using pubs as a venue for facilitating strong bonds and deeper friendships. For women in particular, Thurnell-Read found the pub was somewhere to visit with friends, as part of a wider itinerary of leisure or cultural pursuits such as shopping or visiting an art gallery. Therefore, pubs can also be an important part of maintaining existing friendship networks. The evolution of the role and nature of pubs in recent years has meant that in some cases they can actually function much more like community centres in hosting events and activities that draw in a greater diversity for people. Examples would include yoga sessions, organised talks and film nights. These are all activities that serve to decentre the role of alcohol consumption and by doing so open the pub up to use by a greater diversity of people. This increased diversity enhances the potential for the development of bridging capital, not only between patrons but also between the pub and the wider community itself as it seeks to position itself as a community hub rather than simply a hospitality establishment.

This confirms findings from Cabras and Mounts' (2017) research into the role of the pub in rural Ireland. They argue that pubs are not only the setting for social interactions but also the incubator for a variety of different types of activities which themselves contributed to the social life of a place. Pubs are often the birth place of great ideas (as well as some not so great ones) but Cabras and Mount point to the many community sporting, charity and social events whose inception can be traced back to a discussion in the pub. For this reason, participants in Cabras and Mounts study rated pubs as the strongest facilitator of socialising and engagement locally when compared with other places such as community centres and churches. It should be noted, however, that this study focused on rural communities where the pub was often the centre, if not the whole, of the local economy. Therefore, the position of pubs as a social incubator may be considered even more vital.

Of course, despite the best efforts of many pubs to reposition themselves within the landscape of community social infrastructure, there will still be certain sections of the population who will be excluded. There are still connotations with certain types of gendered identities in pubs that can work to exclude women, for example, and men who do not identify with particular versions of masculinity often present within local drinking cultures. Some pubs are often aimed at certain clientele, sometimes at students and sometimes at 'locals' with the associated exclusion of others. In addition, many migrant communities and minority ethnic communities for whom the consumption of alcohol is either prohibited or not part of their cultural practices may not consider the pub a space of socialising at all. It would also be remiss not to acknowledge the role pubs can play in promoting anti-social behaviour as well as the more positive social interactions discussed above. Cabras and Mount (2017) found that there was a marked gender difference in perceptions of anti-social behaviour in pubs with women being more likely than men to cite this as a problem. This is corroborated by other studies and it would therefore seem reasonable to suggest that such perceptions may discourage some older people from frequenting certain pubs, therefore furthering their social exclusion from these spaces.

INFORMAL AND UNASSUMING: SPACES OF EVERYDAY INTERACTIONS

Whether independently owned or part of a chain, commercial venues offer important spaces of social interaction for older people and each category of space has a role to play as social infrastructure. They are particularly relevant for those older people who may feel excluded from or simply do not identify with more organised forms of socialising offered by formal community activities. They can offer an informal space of social interaction with others where there is little or no expectation and people can come and go as they please at any time. An important theme in this area of research around how older people engage with commercial and hospitality spaces has been around their relationships with the staff at these establishments and the benefits that these specific social connections can bring. Gardner (2011) refers to these connections as relationships of service, where they are based upon one person being part of the service provision for another. These types of relationships are often based on weak ties in that they are relationships that typically only exist within the context of the service being offered and the commercial establishment in which it occurs. This means that although you may exchange friendly pleasantries with a particular barrister in your local coffee shop, you may even know their name and where they are going on holiday, you might not know anything more personal about them and you certainly would not imagine extending the relationship to outside of the coffee shop or arrange to meet them elsewhere. Despite the perhaps thin level of connection exhibited in these types of relationships, they can be, nonetheless, incredibly important especially for older people. Interactions with staff in shops and hospitality outlets can sometimes be the only form of social contact those who are more socially isolated can have. Commercial venues can therefore provide incredibly important passing places of social connection for older people.

6

EVERYDAY SPACES OF
INTERGENERATIONAL ENCOUNTER

Having made the argument in the previous three chapters of the importance of weak ties and of bridging capital for older people, this chapter specifically focuses on one type of bridging capital – that of intergenerational relationships. These are social connections that exist between people of different generations or between people of very different ages, and for the purpose of this book, the discussion will focus exclusively on intergenerational relationships outside of the family. It will consider those connections between people of different ages that occur in communities and, in doing so, asks what types of social infrastructures are best suited to developing these types of connections. Using the theoretical framing of social infrastructure and encounter introduced in Chapter 2, this chapter argues that we need to better understand the potential of the everyday, mundane and often fleeting social interactions we have in the everyday shared spaces of our neighbourhoods and that these interactions can have a significant impact on intergenerational relations.

INTERGENERATIONAL CONNECTIONS AND RELATIONSHIPS

There is broad agreement within the social gerontology literature, of the benefits of intergenerational relationships, both for the people of different ages within those relationships and for society more generally. Older people have been found to enjoy improved mental and physical well-being through intergenerational contact (Thang, 2001). Studies have found evidence of intergenerational contact increasing social activity, increasing the ability to deal with vulnerabilities and reducing social isolation for older people and younger people have been found to benefit from increased resilience, an enhanced sense of social responsibility and better school results (Hatton-Yeo & Batty, 2011; MacCallum & Palmer, 2006; MacCallum et al., 2010). Community level benefits have also been demonstrated through the building of mutual empathy between different age groups and the challenging of ageist attitudes (Vanderbeck, 2007). Yet, despite the demonstrated benefits of intergenerational connections, we actually know very little about them and how and in particular where they might be formed.

Much of the existing research on intergenerational relationships focuses on relationships within the family (Vanderbeck, 2007). Here discussions are often in the context of caring for the older person in such relationships (Stewart, Browning, & Sims, 2015). This body of work limits the discussion of care to a private and domestic sphere without taking into consideration the extended networks of care, both formal and informal, provided throughout the wider community. It also tends to place the older person in a position of dependency. Where research has branched outside of the family unit, to include intergenerational relationships between friends and neighbours, it still tends to be in reference to the caregiving element of the relationship on the part of the younger person. Once again this reinforces notions of dependency and of unidirectional caregiving.

There is a small body of work that considers intergenerational friendships which demonstrates how both the older and younger parties benefit from such relationships (see Elliot O'Dare, Timonen, & Conlon, 2017). An interesting addition to this discussion comes from Vanderbeck's (2007) work on queering generations (see Halberstam, 2005) that challenges the discrete division of generations and implicit intergenerational conflict that can often be assumed in heteronormative research. This work draws attention to the intergenerational solidarity that can be found between people of all ages who share the same identity of sexuality or experience.

However, there is very little empirical discussion of *where* and in what specific settings outside of the domestic sphere, intergenerational connections might be developed. Conversely, the use of public space by those of different ages has often focused on the tensions and conflicts that can arise from intergeneration encounter (see Pain, 2005). Although an awareness of the potential negative aspects of intergenerational encounter is important, Hopkins and Pain (2007) observe that more positive community-based experiences are less well-documented in the literature.

Within policy circles, there has been a growing interest in intergenerational practice (IGP) and intergenerational shared sites. The Beth Johnson Foundation defines IGP as aiming to bring people from different generations together in purposeful, beneficial activities building on the positive resources that different generations have to offer one another (Granville, 2002). Mentoring and tutoring schemes and young children visiting nursing homes are common examples of IGP (Granville, 2002). UK examples of creating spaces for intergenerational encounter include co-locating libraries with children's centres, purposefully designing parks and outdoor space with intergenerational equipment and co-locating different age-related activities in the same community centre (see Melville & Bernard, 2011). Housing design has also been the focus of work on intergenerational encounter. In Germany, Ammann and Heckenroth (2012) surveyed a number of urban housing developments aimed at promoting interactions between people of different ages by purposely designing ways in which they could live alongside each other. Their survey found that collaboration across the community, involving a range of stakeholders representing the interests of different age groups, was vital to the design of intergenerational space.

However, whilst studies of intentionally designed intergenerational spaces and programmes are useful in supporting the argument that these relationships are important, the fact that they are studies of planned spaces, designed specially to orchestrate social encounters, is somewhat limiting. These studies are not able to tell us about the unplanned and spontaneous encounters people of different ages have with one another through their use of public and community spaces in the course of their normal, everyday lives. This chapter argues that discussions of community-based intergenerational encounter would benefit from a greater awareness of the role of community social infrastructures to allow for more attention to be paid to the mundane encounters that occur in everyday spaces.

EVERYDAY ENCOUNTERS ACROSS DIFFERENCE

Intergenerational relationships can be understood as an example of bridging social capital, i.e., it is about developing social networks and connections between those from different age groups. As we have already established there is a lack of empirical research on these types of everyday intergenerational encounters, however, there is a large body of work on everyday inter*cultural* encounters from the well-established area of literature from social and cultural geography concerned with encounter and spaces of encounter in the context of ethnic and cultural diversity. In considering how encounters with cultural diversity can become meaningful (to the extent that they have the potential to foster change), scholars emphasise the need for people to interact with those who are from different backgrounds from them on a regular basis. They also emphasise the importance of proximity and that these interactions need to take place in the localities in which people live. Although much of the work on intercultural encounter does not explicitly engage with the concept of third places, there are strong echoes here of Oldenburg and Bissett's (1982) assertion that third places are local places in which people are able to come into contact with others and that these spaces play a key role socialising in allowing us to become familiar with difference in various forms. As this chapter is particularly interested in the types of intergenerational connections that develop in community settings, we can also use Granovetter's concept of weak ties to think about how these connections are formed through everyday encounter. This is helpful in thinking about what types of interactions are important for building up trust between those of different ages living in the same neighbourhood.

Everyday interactions in everyday spaces can provide important sites and practices of what Gibson-Graham refer to as the 'unwitting, involvement in the practice of collectivity' (2003, p. 65). This becomes particularly important in highly individualised or segregated communities and therefore has an important role to play in intergenerational relations. Therefore, even fleeting encounters can be vital for building the weak ties of association between individuals and groups from different backgrounds. It is these weak ties that provide bridges into other social worlds and can provide the foundation for further trust, knowledge and understanding. However, encounters across difference of any type need to be *meaningful* and can only be so if they actually change values for the people involved in a positive and progressive way (Valentine, 2008). The emphasis on meaningful encounters does not always mean such interactions have to be particularly in-depth or, on their own, have huge significance. The meaningfulness of these encounters comes from the social capital they produce and the possibilities this social capital can have. Informal social interactions can form the basis for the development of greater intergenerational understanding and informal networks of support.

SOCIAL INFRASTRUCTURES OF INTERGENERATIONAL RELATIONSHIPS

So, what social infrastructures might best facilitate these types of interactions? Here, we need to think about the community third places that may or may not have a primary social function but where 'naturally occurring' mundane interactions take place. We also need to think beyond spaces that are typically associated with one age group, such as schools or day centres. Public libraries provide a good example of where intergeneration encounters can take place in communities;

> *After all, places like libraries are saturated with strangers, people whose bodies are different, who make different sounds, speak different languages, give off different, sometimes noxious smells. Spending time in public social infrastructure requires learning to deal with these differences in a civil manner.*
>
> *(Klinenberg, 2018, p. 45)*

Here, Klinenberg points to the important socialisation role libraries play for the wider community. However, we should also consider places such as shops, cafes, public transport and green space, spaces that all age groups use, albeit in perhaps different ways. Places are defined by their ordinariness and unassuming nature (Finlay, Esposito, Hee Kim, Gomez-Lopez, & Clarke, 2019).

Taking an infrastructural approach to intergenerational connections and relationships allows us to understand how these everyday and the ordinary spaces in our communities shape such encounters. This is increasingly important in the context of reduced state funding as targeted programmes of intergeneration practice can demand high levels of co-ordination, support and resources (Buffel et al., 2014). In the context of limited resources, it is prudent to also invest in time and energy in the social infrastructure that already exists in our neighbourhoods that has an equally important part to play in facilitating integrational encounter. Public services in our communities, such as libraries, have been greatly affected by cuts to public funding and as a result may not be able to offer the extended opening times and diversity of services that are essential in drawing in people of different ages. Therefore, it may be commercial spaces such as retail and hospitality that become important passing places of intergenerational encounter. As we have seen in the previous chapter, relationships of service (Gardner, 2011) or commercial relationships (Stones, 1954) can be hugely beneficial for older people. Therefore, we need much more empirical research into how everyday third spaces provide social, functional and care roles in the community and how these might be best supported.

7

PRESSURES ON SOCIAL INFRASTRUCTURE: URBAN DEVELOPMENT, AUSTERITY AND THE CORONAVIRUS PANDEMIC

Hopefully, the discussions in this book so far have made the case of the importance of social infrastructure in supporting the social connections of older people and therefore the critical role these spaces play in age-friendly communities. However, social infrastructure does not exist in a vacuum. It is subject to social, economic and political contexts resulting in an uneven geography of social infrastructures and an unequal capacity within local neighbourhoods to provide the quality and range of infrastructure needed to support ageing in place for a diversifying ageing population. Social infrastructure requires support and investment and in many cases is precariously under threat from a multitude of different forces acting on our cities and communities. This chapter considers some of those pressures in order to give a clearer sense of some of the challenges facing these vital parts of our local communities.

Three main pressures acting on social infrastructure will be considered. Firstly, urban development and regeneration. This can bring about changes to the social infrastructure of a place which will unavoidably impact the lives of the older people who use those spaces. Secondly, is austerity, in the form of the scaling back of the welfare state and other forms of public investment, which has been identified as a key threat to the effectiveness of age-friendly policies more broadly (Buffel & Phillipson, 2016). This chapter discusses the impact austerity might have on the capacity of local communities to be age-friendly with a particular focus on how austerity has impacted on the social infrastructures that support older people. And finally, the year 2020 has meant that any discussion of shared neighbourhood spaces must also consider the impacts of a global pandemic. The final section of this chapter reflects on how social distancing measures have affected the social well-being of different groups of older people and how the impact of the coronavirus pandemic might influence how we use public spaces for some time to come.

URBAN DEVELOPMENT AND REGENERATION

Urban development can mean the investment in residential developments through the building of housing, the regeneration of new retail and leisure spaces through the provision of new shops, services and amenities and business-led investment usually centring on the building of new office space. Urban regeneration can bring many benefits to older people living in more economically marginalised neighbourhoods as it may result in increased investment in infrastructure, new amenities and improved access to services (Smith, Lehning, & Kim, 2018). However, studies have also found that urban regeneration can have negative consequences for existing social infrastructures and may result in the *disinvestment* of social infrastructures that are important to older people or the removal of these places altogether (Buffel & Phillipson, 2019). What is more, the social infrastructure developed in its place may not always be suited to the needs of older existing residents as urban regeneration tends to meet the needs of certain age groups at the expense of others (Buffel & Phillipson, 2019). Despite older people often being the most impacted upon by urban regeneration, they are often the least visible in discussions of urban redevelopment meaning that their needs regarding social infrastructure, as well as housing and service provision, are often overlooked. In the drive to attract families and working age households to cities, older people can often be 'erased' from urban planning and rendered invisible in their own communities (Kelley, Dannerfer, & Masarwech, 2018).

Social infrastructure is often implicitly, if not explicitly, the focus of research into the experiences of older people living in neighbourhoods undergoing urban change through their discussions of how spaces outside the home are transformed. Cultural displacement, and feeling that new amenities and services are not 'for them', is a common sentiment identified by the literature on gentrification for existing residents. In their research into a gentrifying neighbourhood in Manchester, UK, Buffel and Phillipson (2019) found that some older residents stopped visiting the local places that had been important to them because they felt that they would be less likely to meet anyone they knew as their friends or acquaintances no longer used them. This demonstrates how older people can become socially excluded from important social infrastructures even when it continues to exist in a neighbourhood.

Several studies in the United States looking at the impact of gentrification on older residents within particular minority ethnic communities had similar findings. Versy (2018), for example, explored how the disinvestment in Black churches in Harlem led to many older African American residents feeling that their community was not as friendly as it had once been leading to a strong sense that their community was changing around them. As a result, studies report older people avoiding these new spaces preferring (where possible) to travel to other areas where there was social infrastructure they felt comfortable in and where they would be able to meet with others. An example of this comes from García and Rúa's (2018) study of a gentrifying neighbourhood in Chicago where they found some older Puerto Rican residents making long bus journeys to meet with friends at a fast-food outlet rather than frequenting one of the many 'trendy' and 'predominantly white' coffee shops that had opened in their neighbourhood.

Travelling to a different neighbourhood would not be an option for residents with either restricted mobility or finances and therefore could result in the further isolation of many older people. In the case of the older Puerto Ricans in García and Rúa's study, the experience of these older people was considered as part of a longer history of displacement through urban renewal. García and Rúa found that despite having finally achieved secure housing tenure, 'displacement still looms large in their daily lives' as insecurities around housing have been replaced by insecurities around being able to make use of the new local amenities in their gentrifying neighbourhood. Having experienced 'serial displacement' in their lives, these older residents were not averse to change, 'their lives had been defined by great change' (p. 56), but they were averse to neglect and exclusion from the public life and shared spaces within their neighbourhoods.

A common concept used to explain how older people experience urban regeneration is Relph's concept of autobiographical insiderness which is used to show how people draw on landmarks and particular spaces to somehow anchor their memories in place and therefore retain a sense of attachment and belonging to it. For example, Lager, Van Hoven, and Huigen (2013) study of a neighbourhood in the Netherlands demonstrates how a sense of nostalgia for a loss of community was expressed through reference to public community life in shared spaces, such as the street, local shops and public spaces. Similarly, Chui's (2008) research in Hong Kong demonstrates how the building of new residential redevelopment resulted in the destruction of personal, psycho-emotional or social links with a familiar environment. This shows important articulations of meaning and value attached to social infrastructures that should not be overlooked. It is also important to note the many and tireless struggles older resident have often been through to try and support or improve the social infrastructure of their neighbourhoods before developers move in (Rúa, 2017). However, some regenerated spaces and buildings do have the possibility to provide a source of ongoing attachment to place. Yarker (2018) found that in some instances older residents living near regenerated waterfronts were able to reclaim these once derelict spaces both physically through walking and emotionally though their use in the telling of their own memories and stories of these spaces.

Therefore, in addition to its functional use as providers of services and a space for meeting, it is important to also acknowledge the emotional significance of social infrastructure and the importance of heritage and the memories attached to shared spaces for older people's sense of belonging and attachment. Urban regeneration needs to create an urban environment that supports the autonomy and equal rights of older people and others (Vanderbeck & Worth, 2014) and we need to preserve and expand the third spaces that support older people, not just so older people have appropriate services and amenities on their doorstep but so that their social participation can continue during the process of redevelopment and to ensure older people are able to fulfil their everyday needs within the wider community. This enables older people to remain visible in their communities (Burns, Lavoie, & Rose, 2012). This may mean developing co-production approaches to involve older residents in the regeneration of their communities that move beyond mainstream methods of consultation. Research carried out into proposed regeneration in North Manchester in the United Kingdom found that although older residents welcomed investment in regenerating their neighbourhood, they were anxious about whether the existing social needs of their community would be met by new developments (Lewis, Hammond, Kavanagh, Phillipson, & Yarker, 2020). Maintaining the physical environment and the opportunities for participation, engagement and to be visible is a key feature of age-friendly urban development (Cho & Kim, 2016). Therefore, any discussion of the role of social infrastructure in age-friendly communities needs to remain vigilant to the potential threat posed by urban development that may have the needs and interests of groups other than older people at its heart (Lewis et al., 2020).

AUSTERITY

The 'age of austerity' has been characterised as a condition of 'enforced or extreme economy', meaning sustained and, at times, sever funding cuts to public services. In the United Kingdom, this period started after the Coalition

Governments Spending Cut Review was announced in 2010. Although the language of 'austerity' is more commonly used in the United Kingdom, similar patterns of financial retrenchment have been witnessed in the majority of Western economies effected by the 2008 global financial crash (see Davies & Blanco, 2017; Donald et al., 2014; Overmans & Timms-Arnold, 2016).

Within countries, however, cuts have not been equally distributed with research pointing to a social, geographical and sectoral unevenness of the impacts of austerity. The increasing pressure towards further privatisation, residualisation and responsibilisation of public services (Penny, 2020) is felt most keenly in those neighbourhoods and local authorities that are already the most exposed through economic decline and restructuring (Featherstone, Cumbers, Mackinnon, & Strauss, 2012). For example, there is growing evidence that austerity measures have hit cities the hardest (Centre for Cities, 2019) encapsulated by the widely used term 'austerity urbanism' (Peck, 2012). There is a geography to this too. The Centre for Cities report in 2012 confirmed that it was cities in the North of England that had particularly suffered the effects of austerity with some seeing a cut in their spending on day-to-day services of up to 40%. In addition to the negative effects of austerity being concentrated on certain places, the effects of austerity are also borne by those social groups already the most disadvantaged (Hastings, Bailey, Bramley, & Gannon, 2017). This is often as a result of spending cuts being concentrated in cities and poorer urban communities, as Peck writes; austerity measures operate downwards 'concentrating both costs and burdens on those at the bottom of the social hierarchy compounding economic marginalisation with state abandonment' (2012, p. 651). This means austerity measures have had the most detrimental impact on the poorest in society as well as to women, older people and those living with disabilities (Ginn, 2013). In an effort to try to protect the most vulnerable, local authorities have had to make tough decisions about where to make the biggest cuts. This has also meant, however, that non-statutory services have often been the first victims of any reduced budgets. Services such as planning, libraries, leisure and culture activities have therefore suffered the most.

Hitchen and Shaw (2019) cite a 2019 Bureau of Investigative Journalism report that showed 12,000 public spaces have been sold off by UK Councils since 2010. This means 12,000 less spaces where local residents have the opportunity for social interactions. The contraction and disappearance of these spaces has seen 478 libraries in England and Wales close since 2010, and a third of Sure Start Children's centres and 603 youth centres close between 2012 and 2016 (Shaw, 2019). In addition, squeezed household budgets have reduced spending in local high streets resulting in the number of 'voids' or store vacancies increasing from 5.4% in 2008 to 14.1% in 2013 (Bamfield, 2013). Therefore, a combination of direct cuts to funding and reduced household spending locally means our social infrastructures have been hit from both directions under austerity, with the private, public and voluntary sectors all suffering albeit in different ways. The Marmot Review published in 2020 summarised the impact on what it termed 'ignored communities', in the following way:

> Over the last 10 years, these ... communities and areas have seen vital physical and community assets lost, resources and funding reduced, community and voluntary sector services decimated and public services cut, all of which have damaged health and widened inequalities. These lost assets and services compound the multiple economic and social deprivations, including high rates of persistent poverty and low income, high levels of debt, poor health and poor housing that are already faced by many residents.
>
> (Marmot, Allen, Boyce, Goldblatt, & Morrison, 2020a, p. 94)

Research into the impacts of austerity on social infrastructure is quick to point out that it is not just the actual closure or removal of community spaces and services that can have an impact. Austerity has had a breadth of implications. Libraries may remain open, for example, but with reduced opening hours, or may rely more heavily on volunteers instead of paid staff to deliver services. Parks will physically remain in communities but scaled back maintenance may result in certain areas becoming unusable through poor access. In addition, changes to the ownership and management of key social infrastructure can have implications for how socially excluded groups engage with a space. Community asset transfers (CATs), for example, involve the transfer of management and/or ownership of public land, buildings and services from local authority ownership to a community organisation or social enterprise for less than the market value. CATs have seen widespread use as local authorities look to remove costly assets from their balance sheets and usually apply to non-statutory services. In England, local authority managed leisure centres, for example, have declined from 25% in 2014 to just 18% in 2018 and since 2012 at least 576 public libraries have been transferred to some type of community trust (Nichols, Findlay-King, & Forbes, 2020). This produces a mixed economy of how public services are managed and delivered with varying impacts on local communities as a result.

Most research on the impacts of austerity for older people focus on the important, yet narrow concerns of cuts to health and social care and to state welfare and pensions. Looking at the impacts of austerity on age-friendly policies through the lens of social infrastructure, however, can give us a much larger and more detailed picture of how austerity is impacting on an ageing population. Public parks, for example, have been identified in this book as vital spaces of social infrastructure for older people and the wider community. Yet they have not escaped the effects of austerity measures. As 'assets' in terms of land value, some local authorities have made the decision to sell off these public spaces. However, an increasing trend has been to find new models of governance and finance for parks that reduce maintenance costs and increase revenue to at least offset some of those costs. Smith (2021) makes a case study of Gunnersbury Park in West London to demonstrate some of these trends in shifting the responsibility for parks from local authorities to civil society and private actors. Gunnersbury Park is perhaps slightly unusual, at least in the United Kingdom, in that it was the third sector, in the form of a Community Interest Company (CIC) that took over management from the local authority. A common assumption is that third sector management would perhaps be preferable to one that was market-orientated, yet Smith found there was still tension between local residents and the CIC over the increasing commercialisation of the park. Events that had once been free became ticketed, spaces for sports needed to be booked in advance and cafés in the park were taken over by corporate chains. All this, along with heightened security and policing of events, led to the financial and symbolic exclusion of local residents. In short, many felt their local park was no longer 'theirs'. This came to a head with the proposal to install a commercial obstacle course playground in the park which, in the eyes of some residents, would have created a two-tiered playground system with those who could not afford the high entry prices for the commercial facility only being able to use the original free playground. Examples such as this show that it is not just the closure of social infrastructure that may affect people's usage of those spaces, but also that changes in their management can also change a place to the extent that local residents may no longer access it in the same way.

Public libraries are another prominent example of the causalities of austerity. However, as with the example of public parks, funding cuts have also meant a change in the running of libraries most notably through the recruitment of volunteers to assist in delivering the service alongside paid staff. Research from Casselden, Pickard, Walton, and McLeod (2019) suggests that there was a 100% increase in the use of volunteers in public libraries in the United Kingdom in the period between 2008/2009 and 2013/2014, as libraries have had to find different ways to cut costs in order to stay open. The findings from Casselden et al.'s study into the use of volunteers in public libraries are interesting as they highlight the impact that seemingly subtle changes to the running of a public service might have when it comes to its function as a space of social infrastructure. They identify a concern over 'institutional classism' (Pateman, 1999) that could result from a predominance of middle-class volunteers in a library and the potential for conflict to arise over the purpose and role of a public library in certain communities.

This concern was raised by Casselden et al. because they found that in their case study the majority of library volunteers did not come from the surrounding community but from more affluent neighbourhoods and that the volunteers themselves tended to be retired professionals. There is a wider problem if library volunteers do not reflect the communities the institution severs (in terms of class or ethnicity) as this may have an impact on the inclusivity of the library and therefore its ability to function as a space of social connection with people of different backgrounds. Although it can be generally agreed that using volunteers to maintain library services is preferable to their closure, more attention could be paid to how this is managed and the wider impacts it might have.

Austerity has also had far reaching consequences for 'the size, shape and reach of the voluntary sector' (Macmillan, 2011). A report from Oxfam in 2012 described the current context of cuts to local authority budgets, reduced household income and increased demand on services, as 'the perfect storm' facing community groups and organisations working in the most deprived communities. There is a troubling lack of detailed empirical evidence of the details of the impact of austerity on voluntary organisations (Clifford, 2017); however, several studies suggest that the impact of austerity on this sector has been felt most keenly in more deprived areas (Clifford, Geyne-Rahme, & Mohan, 2013), with 66% of total cuts reported in the 25% most deprived local authority areas, compared with 7.5% of total cuts to organisations in the 25% least deprived areas (ACEVO, 2011; cited in Jones, Meegan, Kennett, & Croft, 2016).

Community organisations providing services for the most vulnerable in our communities have had to make difficult decisions of their own in order to keep the doors open. This has often meant increasingly relying on volunteers or sessional staff, reduced opening hours, charging for services that had once been free and collaborating more with other organisations. In many instances though this has not been enough, many have had to close for good. For those older people who use them, either as a participant or volunteer, community and voluntary groups are often a lifeline for social contact, help and advice and for physical and mental well-being. Therefore, any restrictions in the ability to access these spaces will be keenly felt.

The impacts of austerity on social infrastructures do not just extend to local authority delivered services. Austerity has meant reductions in household spending power which has implications for local high streets and traditional markets, especially in neighbourhoods which were already experiencing economic deprivation. As a result, many retailers and services have had to reconsider whether their presence on some local high streets is still tenable. This often leads to the closure of bank branches and post offices which disproportionately occur in economically disadvantaged neighbourhoods (see Chapter 4). Therefore, in some instances, local shopping streets are slowly moving from a utility position to one of retail and consumption function, as spaces for everyday needs (such as banking) are replaced with a more leisure-orientated and specialist offering which may or may not meet the needs of older people and existing communities. Carmona et al. (2019) demonstrate this argument by pointing to the decline of many traditional London markets with new public spaces of leisure and retail being designed for the creative classes and excluding other groups. As older people are more likely to spend more time in their local communities, local high streets are vitally important for supporting age-friendly communities. Reports by Age UK (2016) and Citizens Advice UK (2017) suggest that it is older people who are hit the hardest by banks and post office branch closures.

However, just as public spending cuts might shrink and restrain our social infrastructure, there is some evidence that the age of austerity is witnessing the emergence of new social spaces in our communities. Referred to by researchers in this field as the emerging new spaces of care, Power and Hall (2018) point to spaces such as museums, allotments and parks being increasing appropriated by health care services to act as sites of health and well-being. From a social infrastructure perspective, this is interesting as museums have been identified as places with an increasing social inclusion and health and well-being role particularly for marginalised groups (Morse & Munro, 2018). Although this book would argue the expansion of what can be truly used as a community third place is a good thing, we do need to be mindful of the increased responsibility this can place on institutions like museums and ensure they have the right support to be able to fulfil this additional role. It should also be noted that rationalising of services and the increased demand for volunteers have brought increased social participation opportunities for many people. Notwithstanding the barriers many groups face to volunteering, this has at least given some older people the opportunity to become more involved in their communities and increase their social connections.

More often than not, however, austerity has meant the reduction of spaces of social infrastructure available for older people in their communities. Research examining the impacts of austerity on urban neighbourhoods reveals the stark consequences of the loss of social infrastructure for all residents. Concepts such as 'urbicide' (Coward, 2007), slow violence (Pain, 2019), ruin (Shaw, 2019) and 'slow spoiling' (Penny, 2020) capture the deep impacts of austerity over time and the visible effects it can have on the built and social environment. Shaw's work on 'worlding austerity' brings to life the impact on our sense of self and existential well-being of such losses:

> As spatial beings, or physical and mental wellbeing is bound to the landscapes we inhabit. If these landscapes are ruined by government cutbacks – compounding the already violent production of neoliberal space – a deep world of alienation and insecurity can set in.
>
> (2019, p. 971)

This analysis is particularly important in relation to older people who, subject to ageism, cognitive deterioration or decline in mobility, may already be experiencing a loosening in their connection to the world and the neighbourhoods in which they live. Austerity not only means a loss of spaces for social interaction but also a space within which to be visible to society. As Hitchen and Shaw note,

> Austerity is generating a physically shrinking world for millions of people. And the ability for individuals to open up worlds – and let their minds breathe – is hindered. Austerity is suffocating the world of its public vitality – constricting its spaces, encounters, and temporalities.
>
> (Hitchen & Shaw, 2019, p. 3)

It is not surprising then that studies looking into the emotional and psychological impacts of austerity have found that the closure of important community buildings and services can lead to increased social isolation and loneliness for those who use them. Indeed, research by The Young Foundation (Aylott, Norman, Russell, & Sellick, 2012) found that fears of isolation and loneliness dominated discussions they had with disabled people and their carers when confronted with not being able to access day centres and the all-important rest bite they offered.

In their study of resistance to the closure of a public library and Jewish Day Centre for older people, Robinson and Sheldon (2019) found articulations of community ownership and connection to place and heritage from users that are not fully comprehended by economic-based decisions to close community building. They conclude that austerity does not recognise the social value of ordinary community infrastructure (Robinson & Sheldon, 2019), instead the value of such spaces was 'increasingly reduced to logics of exchange' (Skeggs, 2014, p. 112). Cuts to services in poorer communities can have a symbolic impact on local residents too. Hastings et al. (2017) found that cuts to what have been defined as 'place-keeping services' such as street cleaning and park maintenance can lead to a decline in the local environment to the extent where local community members feel forgotten about and abandoned. Over time such feelings can build to a sense of community decline that can have deep and long-lasting impacts on how people feel about where they live.

It is notable that much of the research on the impacts of reductions in social infrastructure as a result of austerity measures tends to focus more on the practical and functional implications for individuals, rather than the social and emotional. Less research attention has focused on the social implications for people when their local library closes, for example, when their leisure centre increases its membership fee. Based on the review of research already presented in this book, however, we can surmise this impact will be significant, especially for older people.

THE CORONAVIRUS PANDEMIC

In March 2020, the World Health Organization confirmed the outbreak of the COVID-19 coronavirus, first identified in China, as a global pandemic. At the time of writing, the global death toll stands at 2.36 million. Around 20% of these deaths were recorded in the United States and nearly 5% in the United Kingdom. The COVID-19 pandemic has exposed stark inequalities in health, gender, age, income, ethnicity and neighbourhood. Clinically, the virus affects some groups more seriously than others. Age was identified as a mobility risk factor early on, with those aged over 70 deemed one of the most at risk from dying or being seriously ill with the virus. However, early studies into the impacts of the virus have shown that even with pre-existing conditions and age taken into consideration, where you live, your ethnicity and your socioeconomic status, all have an impact on the risk of catching the virus and of being seriously ill or dying from it.

The response of governments around the world to try and gain control of the spread of the virus in the early months of 2020 was unprecedented to many of us. Office workers were told to work from home, schools, non-essential retail and hospitality were closed, and stay at home orders were issued.

National lockdowns became part of the daily discourse – a phrase which would have been unthinkable to most only a few months prior. Early lockdowns in the United Kingdom in 2020 meant citizens were told to stay at home and not to socialise with other households. Leaving home was only permitted if working from home was not possible, for exercise, caring responsibilities, essential shopping and for medical purposes. Similar restrictions were enforced in countries across the world.

One aspect that made the experience of the COVID-19 pandemic so unprecedented was the role of social infrastructure during this time. During other types of disaster or crisis, social infrastructure has been shown to play a key and positive role in facilitating a collective response and in many cases has helped mitigate some of the worst impacts. Leisure centres become temporary shelters, streets become meeting places and cafes become community response hubs. Rebecca Solnit, in her book *A Paradise Built in Hell* (2009), has documented the ways in which communities respond to crisis and disaster through their use of shared spaces. In the book she speaks with a man in Nova Scotia about his community's response to a hurricane and subsequent loss of power in 2003. The man describes people coming out into the street to bear witness to the event together; 'not quite a street party', he explains, 'but everyone was out at once – it was a sense of happiness to see everyone even though we didn't know each other' (p. 4). Solnit also considers the documented experiences of the earthquake in San Francisco in 1906. Here she finds examples of spontaneously launched community centres, makeshift soup kitchens and other food distribution points in Golden Gate Park. Solnit also reflects on the community level responses to the 1989 earthquake in San Francisco:

> *The neighbourhood had, during the days the power was off, cooked up all its thawing frozen food, held barbecues in the street… how people from all walks of life had mixed in candlelit bars that became community centres.*
>
> *(2009, p. 5)*

What Solnit draws our attention to with these examples are the new forms of community and solidarity that can arise in the wake of disaster. She argues that such events not only demonstrate the importance of social ties but also that there is power in these community responses to disaster. The rupture these events can cause in daily life can 'return people to public and collective life and undo some of (the) individualisation' of neoliberal, capitalist economies. People come together in a crisis and in doing so new possibilities of community open up. However, many of the examples of community given by Solnit rely on people being able to come together in public spaces and this was one of the main activities that was forbidden, or at least severely restricted in the response to the COVID-19 pandemic.

Social distancing measures instructed us to stay away from these public spaces, and in many cases, forced their closure altogether. In the popular perception at least, shared spaces became the epicentre of the disaster due to the highly infectious nature of the virus. During the pandemic we were all asked to stay at home and were all prevented from using certain parts of the social infrastructure we had taken for granted. In the public discussions of the impact of social distancing restrictions, the focus outside of epidemiology has been on two things: the impact on the economy and the impact on people's mental health. The fact that the latter has received the attention it has is commendable and welcome. One wonders whether any serious discussion of the impact of the virus on our mental well-being would have been so mainstream 20 years ago. Although the societal implications of a mental health epidemic are sometimes referred to, it is more commonly discussed as an issue affecting individuals and their families. Sociologists, however, have drawn attention to the social implications of the response to the pandemic with many arguing the need to pay attention to the looming *social* recession as a result of self-isolation and social distancing measures in our public places. We have all felt the effects of being cut off from the places that are important to us and social networks these places support. But for some groups of older people, the impacts of social distancing and shielding have been particularly acute and early research suggests that older people living in economically deprived neighbourhoods might be feeling the effects of the restrictions of public spaces particularly deeply (Phillipson et al., 2021).

Research on the relationship between the impact of the virus and neighbourhood has positioned the pandemic as the latest in a series of pressures acting on communities after decades of public spending cuts. Just prior to the pandemic taking hold in the United Kingdom, the 2020 Marmot Review reported on increasingly levels of neighbourhood inequality in England and Wales. These inequalities affect all aspects of a neighbourhood, including service provision and the presence and quality of social infrastructure. Due to long-term disinvestment and more recent austerity measures, poorer neighbourhoods are less likely to have amenities such as food shops, post offices and banks within walking distance. They are less likely to have well-maintained parks and green space and are more likely to have seen reductions, if not total closure, of their public libraries. In a more recent report reflecting on inequalities and the pandemic, Marmot argued that *levels of deprivation and health within an area have an enormous impact on mortality rates from COVID-19, and deteriorating conditions in more deprived local areas [taking the example of England] in the years up to 2020, have meant that COVID-19 mortality has been higher than would have been the case if conditions in deprived areas had improved rather than worsened in the years leading up to the pandemic.*

(Marmot, Allen, Goldblatt, Herd, & Morrison, 2020b)

A report from the Northern Health Science Alliance (2020) blames austerity measures for the unequal health and economic impacts of COVID-19, particularly in parts of the North of England which have borne the brunt of reduced local authority budgets. Reductions in public sector spending in local communities have eroded vital social infrastructure, therefore leaving the older people living in these communities facing a 'double lockdown' in being confined to neighbourhoods without adequate service or social infrastructure provision (Horton, 2020).

If we have learned anything from lockdown it is that despite the global connectivity many of us have and despite the multiple ways of connecting with each other virtually, nothing can replace face-to-face interaction and the inability to access public spaces is felt keenly. Something else also became strikingly apparent – the value of what local social infrastructure we had on our doorsteps. During lockdown restrictions that quality of third places within walking distance came into its own as most of us experienced a shrinking in the spatial patterns of our daily lives. Having places near where you lived to be able to see and be part of some form of social life became a lifeline for those fortunate enough to live in such neighbourhoods. Increased isolation was often the result for those who were not.

So, what might the impacts of the pandemic be on social infrastructure and how older people use these spaces? Researchers at the Manchester Urban Ageing Research Group (MUARG) carried out telephone interviews in 2020 with older people living in Greater Manchester who were already considered as socially isolated prior to the pandemic. From this research they identified the significant impact being cut off from important social infrastructure had on older people but also the crucial mediating effect that being able to access some shared spaces had on daily life in lockdown. For those people of faith who regularly visited a place of worship, their closure was felt very hard. There were, however, some evidence that networks of support that developed out of people attending faith-based organisations were an important resource that people were able to draw upon during this time (Phillipson et al., 2021).

We have seen how important community organisations and the groups and activities they provide can be for isolated older people. Their closure in response to social distancing measures left many older people cut off from important sources of social contact. There were also implications for those who volunteered with these organisations. In the United Kingdom, initial guidance was for all those over 70 years old, and those with underlying health conditions, to 'shield' meaning to drastically limit their social contact with others. This meant many older volunteers, who usually considered themselves healthy and active members of their communities, suddenly found themselves being told to stay at home. The MUARG research found this meant many older people suddenly found themselves dependent on others in a way they had not been before with consequences for their self-esteem and well-being. We have already seen some of the impacts of the closure of community and voluntary organisations as a result of funding cuts and austerity. The closures of these important spaces of social infrastructure due to COVID-19 were all together more sudden, brutal and with little or no physical alternative being available to replace them.

With so many of the spaces of social infrastructure closed off during the pandemic, virtual and online spaces took on an increasing important role with many older people accessing online communities of various descriptions. Online communities can be defined as 'computer-mediated places where people come together with others to converse, exchange information or other resources, learn, play or just be with each other' (Petric, 2014; quoted in Kamalpour, Watson, & Buys, 2020, p. 1342). This can include participating in online chatrooms, blogs, message boards, as well as using social networking sites.

In the United Kingdom, nearly half of those aged 75 and older reported being regular Internet users (ONS, 2019); however, there is a lack of data around exactly what older people use the Internet for and how much of this Internet use is about accessing online communities as opposed to less social activities such as online shopping, for example. Research from Ofcom (2017) in the United Kingdom found that half of Internet users aged 65–74 have a social media profile (2017) and data from research in the United States suggests that around half of adults aged 60 and over use social media suggesting some form of engagement with online communities. This type of data still leaves question marks as to how actively engaged older people are in this online communities.

Emerging research into the experiences of the pandemic for older people suggests a mixed picture when it comes to how older people have engaged with online communities during the pandemic. Research from Phillipson et al. (2021) found that the closure of social spaces and restrictions in visiting people at home meant many older people were often turning to online and digital technologies for the first time to maintain their social connections. Often this was through the telephone, video calls and communication applications such as WhatsApp and mostly to retain connections with family, friends and people they already knew. However, the use of online and digital technologies was also used to access online spaces of community. The same study found older people of faith making use of online technologies to maintain contact with their faith-based groups whilst churches and mosques were closed. For some this allowed them to connect with their religious community at an international scale leading to increased social interaction, whilst others reported missing the face-to-face sociality of their locally based faith-based networks that virtual services were not able to reproduce. The transferring of many community organisation activities online meant that those who had access to and were able to use online technologies were still able to maintain involvement in these communities. Examples included virtual craft groups, online book clubs and exercise sessions.

For those older people who use them, there are important social benefits for engaging with online communities. These virtual spaces allow people to connect with those who have similar interests (Loane, 2015), feel part of a community (McClain, Gullatt, & Lee, 2018, p. 296), access and become involved with leisure and recreational activities offline (Sherbourne & Stewart, 1991) and reduce social isolation and feelings of loneliness (Choi et al., 2014). Kamalpour, Watson, and Buys (2020) have argued that the social networks developed through these virtual spaces, and the access to support the information they provide, can be important for the resilience of older people. Whilst participants in the MUARG study appreciated the opportunities online spaces provided to remain connected to their social networks during this time, for many it was a temporary solution whilst physical spaces of social infrastructure were closed and many were looking forward to being able to return to face-to-face activities when they could. This supports much of the existing literature on older people's engagement with online communities which finds many older users using online communities as a conduit to in-person connections (Harley, Howland, Harris, & Redlich, 2014).

Of course, many older people do not have the option of accessing online communities, whilst others simply do not want to. Digital exclusion remains an important barrier to older people engaging in virtual communities and should be an important consideration in any age-friendly recovery post-pandemic. Advocates of services for older people have raised concerns over a 'digital by default' agenda from many public services arguing this will serve to further marginalise the most excluded older people in our communities. Likewise as much as online spaces of social connection have proved a lifeline for many during the pandemic, current research suggests a strong preference for face-to-face interaction over virtual interaction and this will be especially important if we are to rebuild the sociality of our communities.

Other axis of marginalisation meant that older people from minority ethnic groups experienced social distancing measures in different ways. Research has found that older people from some minority ethnic groups often travel considerable distances outside their local neighbourhoods in order to visit specialist food retailers and culturally specific markets (Yarker, 2020). Some of these markets faced initial restrictions in opening; however, even once they were fully open, many older people were not able to visit them due to fears of using public transport or because they were shielding. These retail spaces were not only important for social contact but also for remaining connected to a sense of shared cultural heritage and identity. Therefore, the implications of being cut off from this social infrastructure has the potential to be damaging to the health and well-being of many older people.

Further research is needed to explore how the COVID-19 pandemic has impacted on older people's relationship to social infrastructure. However, based on emerging evidence and what we already know about the importance of social contact in shared spaces for older people, it is safe to assume the isolating and detrimental effects to health and well-being for many older people of being cut off from their sources of social interaction. Access to our social infrastructure has become central to managing the pandemic, and with the effects being felt so deeply and so widespread, it is reasonable to assume the effects on our public spaces and how we use them will be felt for many years to come.

THE UNEVEN GEOGRAPHY OF SOCIAL INFRASTRUCTURE

Societal changes become written into the brickwork of our cities and communities, and the fortunes of a place, both good and bad, are evident in our public spaces. In calling for a more critical engagement of the age-friendly movement with theories of urban change, Buffel and Phillipson (2016) urge the age-friendly approach to develop policies which can prevent or reduce inequalities associated with urban living. This is no doubt a tall order especially in light of the pressures of austerity, urban change and COVID-19 outlined above. However, as the discussions in this book have hopefully shown, social infrastructure has a critical role to play at the heart of this, not just in creating positive environments in which to age but also in developing inclusive environments for all community members. Without these spaces, we run the risk of further excluding marginalised groups from their communities and disenfranchising them from wider society.

This becomes even more pressing in the context of a recovery from the coronavirus pandemic. Our cities and communities must retain the ability to provide opportunities for encountering difference and for the mixing of people from different backgrounds. Social distancing measures intended to keep us safe from the virus may have unintended consequences for community cohesion and therefore our social infrastructures must be supported to find innovative and safe ways to facilitate social interaction in this new context. The consequences of not doing so may deepen community inequality and division from which it will be difficult to recover. We cannot assume that all neighbourhoods have the capacity to provide the quality and diversity of social infrastructures we need and therefore we must remain vigilant to pressures acting on our communities that might undermine this and challenge these threats wherever possible. In the final chapter of this book, we consider how some of these challenges might be met.

8

AN INFRASTRUCTURAL APPROACH TO AN AGE-FRIENDLY RECOVERY

Social infrastructure is essential in the social recovery from the coronavirus pandemic for promoting social connections, for community cohesion and for continuing to support age-friendly communities. This book has demonstrated the wide diversity of social infrastructures in our neighbourhoods and the different types of social interactions and connections they help produce. The need to focus on protecting and supporting the spaces in our communities that allow us to have social interactions is now even more pressing. This final chapter will reiterate the key conclusions drawn from the reviews of literature on social infrastructures in the previous chapters before setting out a new research agenda around social infrastructure and ageing and how research, policy and practitioners might go about developing an infrastructural approach to an age-friendly recovery from COVID-19 in Western economies.

AN ECOSYSTEM OF SOCIAL INFRASTRUCTURE FOR AGE-FRIENDLY COMMUNITIES

Although all social infrastructures have the capability of supporting a variety of different types of social connections, the literature reviewed in this book has demonstrated that some social infrastructure lend themselves to supporting certain types of social relationships better than others. Outside venues such as parks, community gardens and other types of publicly accessible green space as well as other types of public space have been found to be helpful in facilitating the types of fleeting and everyday interactions that can develop weak social ties and bridging capital. That these spaces are open to use for different purposes and at varying times of the day means that they draw in a diversity of people of different ages, cultural backgrounds, identities and experiences. It is the diversity of users in these outside venues that has the potential for the formation of bridging capital between individuals and groups. The unstructured nature of these spaces – the fact that they are open to be used in a variety of different ways and with no planned organisation – means the interactions within these spaces are unstructured too. People may say hello and acknowledge one another or simply just see each other and therefore the types of social interactions here can be best defined as weak ties.

The social infrastructures of organised activities can produce quite different types of social connections mainly due to the way these infrastructures are used and who uses them. Being part of a religious organisation, for example, or a sports group or volunteering at a food bank all require some level of commitment and some degree of regularity in attendance even if this varies over time. Being part of these organised activities also means coming together with others for a similar or shared purpose, such as to practice a shared religion together, partake in a sporting activity together or volunteer with the same charity, for example. This coming together with others for a shared purpose or because of shared backgrounds, values or interests provides a bond of commonality between people. The regularity with which these social infrastructures are accessed means this bonding capital has the potential to form strong bonds between people. Of course, visiting a church every Sunday does not mean you will become close friends with every member of the congregation, and a volunteer at a food bank will not develop deep friendships with every other volunteer there, but the way in which these social infrastructures function, and the types of people they draw in, at least provides the possibilities for some strong bonds of friendship to develop and where they do not there is still the potential for weak ties to develop.

The activities that occur within public services such as libraries and schools can be similar especially if they include programmed activities designed to bring people together. But the variation in how both schools and libraries operate and the lack of detailed research into the social lives of these places as community infrastructure make it more difficult to draw a general conclusion. Certainly, however, libraries have been identified in this book as important spaces for the social lives of their communities as they are open to all and offer an unstructured environment for everyone to use either solitarily or socially. It is this diversity of users that heighten a public library's capacity for facilitating bridging capital within the community. Although schools and other educational institutions have their primary focus on their students and pupils, their position within the wider community has been growing and therefore leaves them very well positioned to contribute to the same types of bridging social connections as libraries do.

Commercial venues might have been the least obvious of the social infrastructures discussed in this book; however, due to their position in our communities as everyday spaces that most people have a need to use at some point and to some extent, they are perfectly positioned to facilitate social interactions between people of different backgrounds and experience. This book has defined such spaces as passing places. A review of the research around how older people socialise in hospitality venues found a number of studies pointing to the importance of chain cafes and food outlets. The ability of these spaces to create informal, relaxed and, at times, more inclusive environments meant that older people felt they could make it their own and socialise there in the way they wanted to. This meant being able to drop in and out of social groups as they wished and without any obligation or expectation. Weak ties were made with others but they were important ones that created a sense of familiarity and belonging. Interactions with staff in both hospitality and retail spaces were shown to be particularly important for older people. The regularity with which some older people interact with market traders, for example, or cashiers in the local bank creates important networks of support that can kick into action when required whilst also providing an important sense of familiarity and continuity for people in their communities. As commercial venues are social infrastructures used by all of us to some extent, their ability to draw in a diversity of people across the immediate neighbourhood and further afield means commercial spaces do have the potential to develop bridging social capital between individuals and groups from different backgrounds. This bridging capital tends to be developed through weak ties of association and acquaintances but can be nonetheless very important in reducing community tension and promoting cohesion over time.

Older people, like any other age group, need a mix of different types of social relationships and connections. Having good quality, strong friendships is important, but so too is having acquaintances to acknowledge and say hello to as is the ability to recognise familiar faces where you live. The strength of weak ties connects people to places and communities and gives them access to different social networks outside of their usual social circles. Whilst this book does not want to argue that some types of social capital are more important than others, it does want to stress that we should not overlook the crucial importance of weak ties, especially for older people. These weak ties provide important connections to place and communities that require little or no effort or obligation. They can act as bridges into other social worlds and therefore can give older people access to information and support they otherwise may not have had.

If we recognise our need to have a diversity of social connections in our lives, then we must also recognise the need to have a diversity of social infrastructures that can facilitate these connections. We therefore need an ecosystem of social infrastructures including spaces that allow for groups and individuals to come together in organised activity as well as those more unstructured and everyday passing places of socialisation where people have social interactions that are more unplanned and informal.

A NEW RESEARCH AGENDA – AN INFRASTRUCTURAL APPROACH TO AGE-FRIENDLY COMMUNITIES

As quality of life and well-being concerns have moved up the ageing agenda policy and research have responded by emphasising the building of social connections for older people. This, however, has occurred without a clear understanding of the types of social connections required for ageing well or what space and places in community can actually support the development of these connections. The conceptual framework of social infrastructure provides a way of working towards this and the second part of this concluding chapter will set out a new research agenda around social infrastructure and ageing.

An infrastructural approach to age-friendly communities will need to carefully consider the four following points;

(1) The need for more research into *everyday intergenerational interactions* and the spaces in our communities in which these occur.

(2) The need for new and *innovative research methodologies* for exploring social infrastructure and the importance of involving older people in co-research and co-design.

(3) The need for more research into the types of social infrastructure that are important to *different groups* within the older population.

(4) A greater appreciation of how *inequalities* produce an uneven geography of social infrastructure and shape people's access to and experience of shared spaces.

*The need for more research into **everyday intergenerational interactions** and the spaces in our communities in which these occur.*

As demonstrated in Chapter 6, we have a lack of detailed understanding of how intergenerational relationships are developed outside of the family and in neighbourhood spaces. Social infrastructure provides a framework with which to start exploring this more. A particularly beneficial area of study would be the everyday encounters between different generations that occur in everyday spaces in our community. This would complement, and extend, the more established field of research into intentional and planned intergenerational work that evaluates the success of intergenerational programmes or the intergenerational design of buildings and services. Whilst the latter area of work is important, it only gives us a partial picture of how intergenerational interactions and connections work in a community setting. The study of ageing and of intergenerational interactions in particular has much to learn from looking to research on everyday convivialities and encounters between those of different cultural backgrounds. As older populations become increasingly diverse in terms of ethnicity, cultural background and migration status, questions of intergenerational relationships outside of the family cannot be separated from questions of intercultural encounter (Yarker, 2021).

*The need for new and **innovative research methodologies** for exploring social infrastructure and the importance of involving older people in co-research and co-design.*

An infrastructural approach to ageing requires us to think about new and innovate research methodologies that can get to the fine grain detail of how older people use social infrastructures, what interactions they have there, what these interactions mean to them and how they shape the experience of ageing. As has been seen in the review of many of the studies presented in this book, research can often stop short of examining the detail of social interactions and relationships. We need to know much more about whether people are developing weak connections or strong ones and who these connections are with. Are they based upon a sense of a common bond between individuals or groups, or are they encounters with difference? If they are the latter, the study of ageing would benefit greatly from a greater understanding of what conditions might provide the opportunities for meaningful encounter with difference and therefore what might facilitate wider community connections. More qualitative-based studies and ethnographic accounts of everyday life in neighbourhoods for older people would be useful here, but researchers should also be bold with their methodological choices and engage with more experimental methods such as photo elicitation, walking interviews and documentary making. Such methodologies could usefully learn from a large and growing body of work in ageing studies around co-production and the importance of involving older people in both the co-design and co-research around social infrastructure (Buffel, 2015).

*The need for more research into the types of social infrastructure that are important to **different groups** within the older population.*

Developing on from a call for a continued engagement with methods of co-production is the need for much further research into the types of social infrastructures that are important for different groups of older people. In many Western societies, the population is not only growing older but also growing increasingly diverse. Older people from different religious and ethnic backgrounds, different migratory statuses, people with different health conditions, disabilities and mobility issues and those who identify with more marginalised groups such as LGBTQ+ will all have different types of social infrastructure that are important to them or, conversely, that they feel excluded from. A Muslim man, for example, might cite a local mosque as a particularly important site for social interaction with others. Yet if the same mosque were to host an event for the wider community, a gay man from the white British community might be hesitant to attend and feel unsure as to whether or not he would be welcome. Instead, he might prefer to travel some distance to attend a social event hosted by an equalities and diversity third-sector organisation. A Muslim man may also not consider the local pub as a place where he could meet friends, but for others, the pub would be the ideal place to catch up with friends. Whilst we can make these broad assumptions around what social infrastructures might be important to older people of different backgrounds and identities, we need to know much more and in much greater detail if we are to be able to support the social connections of people ageing in their communities. A future research agenda taking an infrastructural approach to age-friendly communities needs to get both specific and general. It needs to draw upon the long history of community studies to understand how neighbourhoods work for those who are ageing there but it also needs to consider the different needs of different groups of older people and how these are changing. One way of doing this would be to engage further with co-production methods, working with different groups of older people themselves and organisations working with different communities to ensure what is important to older people is at the heart of any research on social infrastructure and ageing.

*A greater appreciation of how **inequalities** produce an uneven geography of social infrastructure and shape people's access to and experience of shared spaces.*

As we saw in Chapter 7, social infrastructures are not naturally occurring and do not exist in a vacuum. They are subject to social, economic pressures and, as such, the capacity for neighbourhoods to support the diversity of social infrastructure needed is uneven. Those places which are better resourced when it comes to infrastructures such as public libraries, bank branches, parks and busy high streets are more likely to be found in higher income neighbourhoods. Consequently, the effects of cuts to public services and reductions in household spending are likely to be felt first, and more keenly, in lower income areas where social infrastructures may already be under pressure. A study of social infrastructure then allows us to also study the effects of inequality on neighbourhoods and responds to the call from Latham and Layton (2019) by taking an infrastructural approach towards a politics of provision. Such an approach will also contribute to a call in the wider age-friendly literature for a more serious engagement of policy and research with issues of structural inequalities. What is often lacking from these debates is an explicit understanding of how wider structural inequalities can undermine the capacity of a neighbourhood to support ageing in place effectivity and to the standards by which older people can enjoy a good quality of life and well-being (Buffel & Phillipson, 2018). As of the year 2020, any discussion of inequalities will need to acknowledge the impact of the coronavirus pandemic. The pandemic so far has already highlighted, and exacerbated, inequalities between our neighbourhoods as well as health inequalities within national populations. Therefore, we might add pandemic planning to the list of pressures already identified by Buffel and Phillipson (2016) as acting on age-friendly cities in the twenty-first century and to what we need to consider in future age-friendly research and policy.

POST-PANDEMIC INFRASTRUCTURES

As we move out of the coronavirus pandemic and into a period of recovery, we stand at a crucial point in history to be able to make real and meaningful changes to how we plan our cities and communities. Many disasters such as flooding and earthquakes require significant rebuilding of infrastructure. Roads need to be repaired and flood defences re-evaluated. Our social infrastructure requires the same attention in the wake of the COVID-19 pandemic. In some cases, it will need rebuilding, if not physically then in terms of its social functions.

Whilst the details of what a post-pandemic world will look like is still being worked out, there seems to be some consensus that building back will need to tackle the issue of inequalities head on. Building back better, fairer and levelling up are some of the narratives coming from the United Kingdom and, promisingly, several reports published in 2020 and 2021 focus on the importance of social infrastructure for rebuilding in a more equitable way. In the United Kingdom, 'levelling up' has become the dominant narrative from central government in how it intends to rebuild from the pandemic. Despite criticism for being somewhat of an ambiguous and confused agenda (Tomaney & Pike, 2020), the commitment to addressing long-term and persistent inequalities within and between UK towns and cities has been welcomed. Levelling up aims to address the persistent geographic economic inequalities in the United Kingdom and to improve the economic positions of towns and cities that so far have been left behind in comparison to the economic buoyancy of the more prosperous parts of the country. In addition to an economic imperative to levelling up, there has also been a strong argument for the social and civic rebuilding of left-behind towns and communities. Social infrastructure has been identified as key in achieving this.

A report for UK government published in 2020 titled *Levelling up our communities: proposals for a new social covenant* identifies social infrastructure as one of the four core principles that should guide a social model of recovery from the pandemic. The report argues that social capital is a crucial pre-requisite to building back better and therefore calls on governments to focus their public spending on places that build social capital, bring people together and facilitate connections within and across communities. This would mean a commitment to modernising and renewing social infrastructure and listening to communities when advocating for important spaces in their neighbourhoods that need saving. The report offers several practical policy innovations to help achieve this, such as ensuring social value is at the heart of commissioning and Community Improvement Districts so that communities would have both the freedom and the responsibility to develop new models of economic and social policy. In agreement with Klinenberg, the report also argues that libraries have a critical role to play in the new social model we need to create and should receive government support in becoming to hub of twenty-first century communities.

As discussed in the introduction to this book, the story of a community is the story of its social infrastructure and when residents see decline and lack of investment in their community assets and amenities, it can amplify feelings of being forgotten and left behind. Restoring social infrastructure will also be an important step to restoring civic and community pride (Kelsey & Kenny, 2021).

Cox and Streeter (2019) point to the 'amenities effect' of living in an area with a high concentration of amenities (defined in their survey as spaces such as parks, libraries, restaurants and shops) and how this can increase our sense of satisfaction with our neighbourhood, make us more likely to remain living there, make us more likely to trust and lend a hand to our neighbours, make use take more of an interest in local events and decrease the chance of experiencing social isolation or feeling lonely.

There are also important economic benefits to investing in social infrastructure, the evidence of which is particularly important as it carries the most weight with government and policy makers (Kelsey & Kenny, 2021). Vibrant high streets, employment and increased skills are some of the economic impacts social infrastructure can have. Calls for re-investing in town centres and local high streets were growing for some time before the pandemic (Portas, 2011). From an economic point of view, vibrant high streets with a diversity of retail, leisure and services increase footfall, revenue and attract further inward investment. Their diversity also provides a more robust local economy more resilient to external shocks (Highstreets Task Force, 2020). Retaining and increasing this diversity of use might require some rethinking from planning to ensure a balance between new commercial and residential developments (Calafati et al., 2019).

Kelsey and Kenny (2021) cite several studies that show social infrastructure can be especially important for youth employment with data from the Office of National Statistics (ONS) showing that 700,000 16–24-year-olds are employed in occupations linked to social infrastructure. This employment is mostly associated with the retail, hospitality and arts and culture sectors, sectors hit particularly hard by social distancing measures. Once again libraries are singled out as social infrastructure of particular importance. Kelsey and Kenny cite research based on the Carnegie Investment programme in the United States showing the positive impact on skills and innovation in areas where the trust has invested in the local library.

Putting social infrastructure at the heart of any post-pandemic recovery plan requires governments to rethink their approach to infrastructure. Instead of prioritising new developments that promote mobility and connectivity between places, the lens of social infrastructure requires us to focus on connection *within* places. If social infrastructure is to play a greater role in recovery from the pandemic, we will need to improve the quality and availability of data about it. Kelsey and Kenny (2021) suggest this could be done by governments working with the ONS to develop a digital repository to bring together data on different community assets and their use. Not only would better data enable better planning, but also it would go some way to social infrastructure achieving parity with 'hard' infrastructure. This would have to be matched with funding and Kelsey and Kenny (2021) recommend government ring-fencing 25% of the Levelling up the Towns fund for investment in social infrastructure.

The experience of the pandemic and social distancing measures may have changed our relationship with online and digital communication forever, and indeed online communities may be an increasingly important social spaces for future older generations. The pandemic has certainly re-emphasised the need to increase efforts to ensure no one (including older people) is left behind by the 'digital imperative' and we must ensure digital inclusion is central to age-friendly work. However, based on existing research around the importance of face-to-face social interactions for older people and the importance of the neighbourhood to this demographic, the rebuilding of physical spaces of social infrastructure must be a priority.

Research on post-pandemic cities has been growing for some time and will no doubt continue to be a focus of even more research to come. Within this re-emerging research agenda, it is imperative that we do not lose sight of age-friendly principles in any post-pandemic planning, design and use of public space. Do to so would risk further entrenching the inequalities brought to light by the pandemic. We must ensure that the shared and public spaces in our communities are allowed to maintain their social functions even if this is not the primary remit of the establishment. They must remain able to facilitate conversation as well as the more casual, fleeting and even non-verbal inter-actions that, as hopefully this book has demonstrated, are so important especially to older people and those who might be socially isolated.

Whatever stage in the life course you might identify with, hopefully in reading this book you have had chance to reflect on your own experiences of social infrastructure, experiences which will no doubt have been changed by the coronavirus pandemic. The poignancy of writing a book in 2020 on the use of public spaces by older people could hardly be overlooked. However, it has also shed a light on the evolving nature of our shared spaces. Even during a period of social upheaval, new spaces of social infrastructure and connection have developed. Small pockets of solidarity emerged on street corners and pavements, in the queues for supermarkets and shops and in online spaces – the latter, already, a vital part of some people's social lives. Social distancing has meant seeing, traversing and inhabiting space in different ways, with those of us lucky enough to be able to access parks and green spaces and using them in ways that perhaps we did not before. Balconies, driveways and doorsteps have become semi-private spaces from which to create a new sense of com-munity. There have been examples of social infrastructures adapting in vital ways. Some pharmacies in the United Kingdom, for example, have been designated as safe places for those experiencing domestic abuse to access support; a sobering reminder that, for many, these third places can often be a safer environment than the 'first' place of home. We have perhaps learned to appreciate different types of social interaction too. A sign put up at a local walking spot in south Manchester in the spring of 2020 urged people to smile and say hello to people as they pass to help others feel less lonely, perhaps the clearest reminder of the importance of weak ties and informal, fleeting interactions. Many more empirical studies of the social impacts of the pandemic will be needed in the future to make sense of this time but one lesson we should be sure to take from the pandemic is that we must value, fight for and protect our often mundane yet critical social infrastructure.

REFERENCES

Abendstern, M., Hughes, J., Jasper, R., Sutcliffe, C., & Challis, D. (2018). Care co-ordination for older people in the third sector: Scoping the evidence. *Health and Social Care in the Community*, 26(3), 314–329.

Nature Editorial A different agenda. (2012). *Nature*, 487, 271. doi:10.1038/487271a

Age UK. (2016). Bank branch closure briefing. Report by Age UK. Retrieved from https://www.ageuk.org.uk/latest-news/archive/bank-branch-closures-a-problem-for-older-people/. Accessed on January 29, 2021.

Alley, D., Liebig, P., Pynoos, J., Banerjee, T., & Choi, I. H. (2007). Creating elder-friendly communities: Preparation for an aging society. *Journal of Gerontological Social Work*, 49, 1–18.

Ambition for Ageing. (2019). *Working inclusively to make communities age-friendly*. Manchester: Greater Manchester Centre for Community and Voluntary Organisation.

Amin, A. (2002). Ethnicity and the multicultural city: Living with diversity. *Environment and Planning A*, 34, 959–980.

Ammann, I., & Heckenroth, M. (2012). Innovations for intergenerational neighbourhoods. *Journal of Intergenerational Relationships*, 10(3), 228–245.

Anderson, E. (2011). *The cosmopolitan canopy: Race and civility in everyday life*. New York, NY: W.W. Norton Company.

Arai, S., & Pedlar, A. (2003). Moving beyond individualism in leisure theory: A critical analysis of concepts of community and social engagement. *Leisure Studies*, 22, 185–202.

Arksey, H., & O'Malley, L. (2005). Scoping studies: Towards a methodological framework. *International Journal of Social Research Methodology*, 8(1), 19–32.

Askins, K. (2016). Emotional citizenry: Everyday geographies of befriending, belonging, and intercultural encounter. *Transactions of the Institute of British Geographers, 41*, 515–527.

Augé, M. (1995). *Non-places: Introduction to an anthropology of supermodernity.* London: Verso.

Aylott, M., Norman, W., Russell, C., & Sellick, V. (2012). *An insight into the impacts of the cuts on some of the most vulnerable in Camden.* A Young Foundation Report for London Borough of Camden.

Bamfield, J. (2013). *Retail futures 2018.* Report for the Centre for Retail Research.

Bedimo-Rung, A. L., Mowen, A. J., Cohen, D. A. (2005). Significance of parks to physical activity and public health: A conceptual model. *American Journal of Preventative Medicine, 23* (2S) 5L 14.

Bolton, M. (2012). *Loneliness: The state we're in.* Report by Age UK.

Booth, L. (2021). *Bank branch and ATM statistics.* House of Commons Briefing Paper. Retrieved from https://researchbriefings.files.parliament.uk/documents/CBP-8570/CBP-8570.pdf

Briggs, A. (1963). *Victorian cities.* Harmondsworth: Penguin.

Broughton, K. A., Payne, L., & Liechty, T. (2017). An exploration of older men's social lives and wellbeing in the context of a coffee group. *Leisure Sciences, 39*(3), 261–276.

Buffel, T. (2015). *Researching age-friendly communities: Stories from older people as co-investigators.* Manchester: Manchester University Library.

Buffel, T., De Backer, F., Peeters, J., Phillipson, C., Romero Reina, V., Kindekens, A., … Lombaerts, K. (2014). Promoting sustainable communities through intergenerational practice. *Social and Behavioural Sciences, 116*, 1785–1791. 21 February.

Buffel, T., & Phillipson, C. (2016). Can global cities be 'age-friendly cities'? Urban development and ageing populations. *Cities, 55*, 94–100.

Buffel, T., & Phillipson, C. (2018). A manifesto for the age-friendly movement: Developing a new urban agenda. *Journal of Aging & Social Policy, 30*(2), 173–192.

Buffel, T., & Phillipson, C. (2019). Ageing in a gentrifying neighbourhood: Experiences of community change in later life. *Sociology, 53*(6), 987–1004.

Burholt, V., Dobbs, C., & Victor, C. R. (2016). Transnational relationships and cultural identity of older migrants. *Geropsychology*, *29*, 57–69.

Burns, V. F., Lavoie, J. P., & Rose, D. (2012). Revising the role of neighbourhood change in social exclusion and inclusion of older people. *Journal of Aging Research, 2012*. doi:10.1155/2012/148287

Cabras, I., & Mount, M. P. (2017). How third places foster and shape community cohesion, economic development and social capital: The case of pubs in rural Ireland. *Journal of Rural Studies*, *55*, 71–82.

Calafati, L., Ebrey, J., Froud, J., Haslam, C., Johal, S., & Williams, K. (2019). *How an ordinary place works: Understanding Morriston*. Foundational Economy Research Report. Retrieved from https://foundationaleconomycom.files.wordpress.com/2019/05/morriston-report-v6-13-may-2019.pdf

Carmona, M., Sandkjær Hanssen, G., Lamm, B., Nylund, K., Saglie, I.-L., & Tietjen, A. (2019). Public space in an age of austerity. *Urban Design International*, *24*, 241–259.

Casselden, B., Pickard, A., Walton, G., & McLeod, J. (2019). Keeping the doors open in an age of austerity? Qualitative analysis of stakeholder views on volunteers in public libraries. *Journal of Librarianship and Information Science*, *51*(4), 869–883.

Centre for Ageing Better. (2018). *Primary research into community contributions in later life*. London: Centre for Ageing Better.

Centre for Cities. (2019). *Cities outlook report*. Retrieved from https://www.centreforcities.org/reader/cities-outlook-2019/

Chang, P.-J., Wray, L., & Lin, Y. (2014). Social relationships, leisure activity, and health in older adults. *Health Psychology*, *33*(6), 516–523.

Cheang, M. (2002). Older adults' frequent visits to a fast-food restaurant: Nonobligatory social interaction and the significance of place in a 'third place'. *Journal of Aging Studies*, *16*, 303–321.

Choi, J., Kim, S., Moon, J. Y., Kang, J., Lee, I., & Kim, J. (2014). Seek or provide: Comparative effects of online information sharing on seniors' quality of life. *Communications of the Association for Information Systems*, *34*(1), 27.

Cho, M., & Kim, J. (2016). Coupling urban regeneration with age-friendliness: Neighbourhood regeneration in Jangsu Village, Seoul. *Cities*, *58*, 107–114.

Chui, E. (2008). Ageing in place in Hong Kong–Challenges and opportunities in a capitalist Chinese city. *Ageing International, 32*(3), 167–182.

Clifford, D. (2017). Charitable organisations, the great recession and the age of austerity: Longitudinal evidence for England and Wales. *Journal of Social Policy, 46*(1), 1–30.

Clifford, D., Geyne-Rahme, F., & Mohan, J. (2013). Variations between organisations, and localities in government funding of third-sector activity: Evidence from the national survey of third-sector organisations in England. *Urban Studies, 50*(5), 959–976.

Conradson, D. (2003). Geographies of care: Spaces, practices, experiences. *Social and Cultural Geography, 4*, 451–454.

Coward, M. (2007). 'Urbicide' reconsidered. *Theory and Event, 10*(2). doi: 10.1353/tae.2007.0056

Cox, D. A., & Streeter, R. (2019). *The importance of place: Neighbour amenities as a source of social connection and trust.* American Enterprise Institute. Retrieved from https://www.aei.org/research-products/report/the-importance-of-place-neighborhood-amenities-as-a-source-of-social-connection-and-trust/

Crow, G. (2018). *What are community studies?* London: Bloomsbury.

Davies, J. S., & Blanco, I. (2017). Austerity urbanism: Patterns of neoliberalisation and resistance in six cities of Spain and the UK. *Environment and Planning A, 49*(7), 1517–1536.

DH. (2016). *Care act statutory guidance.* Department of Health, London. Retrieved from www.gov.uk/goverment/publications/care-act-statutory-guidance. Accessed on June 12, 2016.

Dines, N., & Cattell, V. (2006). *Public spaces, social relations and well-being.* Bristol: The Policy Press.

Dolley, J. (2020). Community gardens as third places. *Geographical Research, 58*(2), 141–153.

Donald, B., Glasmeier, A., Gray, M., Lobao, L. (2014). Austerity in the city: Economic crisis and urban service decline? *Cambridge Journal of Regions, Economy and Society, 7*(1), 3–15.

Doran, P., & Buffel, T. (2018). Translating research into action: Involving older people in co-producing knowledge about age-friendly neighbourhood intervention. *Working with Older People, 22*(1), 39–47.

Draper, C., & Freedman, D. (2010). Review and analysis of the benefits, purposes and motivations associated with community gardening in the United States. *Journal of Community Practice, 18*, 458–492.

Elliot O'Dare, C., Timonen, V., & Conlon, C. (2017). Intergenerational friendships of older adults: Why do we know do little about them? *Aging and Society, 39*(1), 1–16.

Ellor, J. W. (2004). Micro practice and faith-based initiatives: The role of religious congregations in the social service system. *Journal of Religious Gerontology, 16*(1–2), 15–35.

Ellor, J. W., & Coates, R. B. (1986). Examining the role of church in the aging network. *Journal of Religion & Aging, 2*(1–2), 99–116.

Featherstone, D., Cumbers, A., Mackinnon, D., & Strauss, K. (2012). Boundary crossing progressive localism in the age of austerity. *Transactions of the Institute of British Geographers, 37*(2), 177–182.

Fields, N. L., Adorno, G., Magruder, K., Parekh, R., & Felderhoff, B. J. (2016). Age-friendly cities: The role of churches. *Journal of Religion, Spirituality and Aging, 28*(3), 264–278.

Finlay, J., Esposito, M., Hee Kim, M., Gomez-Lopez, I., & Clarke, P. (2019). Closure of 'third-places'? Exploring potential consequences for collective health and wellbeing. *Health and Place, 60*, 102225.

Forrest, R., & Kearns, A. (2001). Social cohesion, social capital and the neighbourhood. *Urban Studies, 38*, 2125–2143.

García, I., & Rúa, M. M. (2018). 'Our interests matter': Puerto Rican older adults in the age of gentrification. *Urban Studies, 55*(14), 3168–3184.

Gardner, P. J. (2011). Natural neighbourhood networks–Important social networks in the lives of older adults aging in place. *Journal of Aging Studies, 25*, 263–271.

Gehl Institute. (2018). Inclusive healthy places: A guide to inclusion and health in public space. Retrieved from https://gehlinstitute.org/wp-content/uploads/2018/07/Inclusive-Healthy-Places_Gehl-Institute.pdf

Genter, C., Roberts, A., Richardson, J., & Sheaff, M. (2015). The contribution of allotment gardening to health and wellbeing: A systematic review of the literature. *British Journal of Occupational Therapy, 78*(10), 593–605.

GHIA. (2019). *Nature and ageing well in towns and cities: Why natural environment matters for healthy ageing.* Report My University of Manchester.

Gibson- Graham, J. K. (2003). An ethics of the local. *Rethinking Marxism*, *15*(1), 49–73.

Ginn, J. (2013). Austerity and inequality: Exploring the impact of cuts in the UK by gender and age. *Research on Ageing and Social Policy*, *1*(1), 28–53.

Glover, T. D. (2018). All the lonely people: Social isolation and the promise and pitfalls of leisure. *Leisure Sciences*, *40*(1–2), 25–35.

Goheen, P. (1998). Public space and the geography of the modern city. *Progress in Human Geography*, *22*, 479–496.

Gonzalez, S., & Waley, P. (2012). Traditional retail markets: The new gentrification frontier? *Antipode*, *45*(4), 965–983.

Granovetter, M. S. (1973). The strength of weak ties. *American Journal of Sociology*, *78*(6), 1360–1380.

Granville, G. (2002). *A review of intergenerational practice in the UK*. Stoke-on-Trent: Beth Johnson Foundation.

Gray, A. (2009). The social capital of older people. *Ageing and Society*, *29*(1), 5–31.

Habermas, J. (1989). *The structural transformation of the public sphere*. Cambridge: Polity Press.

Halberstam, J. (2005). *In a queer time and place: Transgender bodies, subcultural lives*. New York, NY: New York University Press.

Halpern, D. (2005). *Social capital*. Cambridge: Polity Press.

Harley, D., Howland, K., Harris, E., & Redlich, C. (2014). Online communities for older user: What can we learn from local community interactions to create sites that work for older people. In Proceedings of the 28th International BCS Human Computer Interaction Conference. Retrieved from https://www.semanticscholar.org/paper/Online-communities-for-older-users%3A-what-can-we-to-Harley-Howland/3d7b1612247e1ffbaad6a6ffdbe12f85883d81ee

Haslam, S. A., Jetten, J., Postmes, T., Haslam, C. (2009). Social identity, health and wellbeing: AN emerging agenda for applied psychology. *Applied Psychology: International Review*, *58*(1), 1–23.

Hastings, A., Bailey, N., Bramley, G., & Gannon, M. (2017). Austerity urbanism in England: The 'regressive redistribution' of local government services and the impact on the poor and marginalised. *Environment and Planning A, 49*(9), 2007–2024.

Hatton-Yeo, A., & Batty, C. (2011). Evaluating the contribution of intergenerational practice. In P. Ratcliffe & I. Newman (Eds.), *Promoting social cohesion, implications for policy and evaluation*. Bristol: Policy Press.

Hauser, C., Tappeiner, G., & Walde, J. (2007). The learning region: The impact of social capital and weak ties on innovation. *Regional Studies, 41*(1), 75–88.

Heley, J., & Jones, L. (2013). Growing older and social sustainability: Considering the 'serious leisure' practices of the over 60s in rural communities. *Social and Cultural Geography, 14*(3), 276–299.

Heley, J., Jones, L., & Yarker, S. (2020). Retiring into civil society. In S. Power (Ed.), *Civil society through the lifecourse*. Bristol: Policy Press.

Hickman, P. (2013). Third places and social interaction in deprived neighbourhoods in Great Britain. *Journal of Housing and the Built Environment, 28*(2), 221–236.

High Streets Task Force. (2020). *Review of high street footfall*. July 2019–June 2020. Retrieved from https://www.highstreetstaskforce.org.uk/media/b5dnkp4z/hstf-footfall-report-2020-for-publication.pdf

Hitchen, E., & Shaw, I. G. R. (2019, March 7). *Intervention–'Shrinking worlds: Austerity and depression'*. AntipodeFoundation.org.

Holland, C., Clark, A., Katz, J., & Peace, S. (2017). *Social interactions in urban public places. A report for the Joseph Rowntree Foundation*. London: Policy Press.

Holt-Lunstad, J., Smith, T. B., & Layton, J. B. (2010). Social relationships and mortality risk: A meta-analytical review. *PLoS Medicine, 7*(7).

Hong, A., Sallis, J. F., King, A. C., Conway, T. L., Saelens, B., Cain, K. L., ... Frank, L. D. (2018). Linking green space to neighbourhood social capital in older adults: The role of perceived safety. *Social Science and Medicine, 207*, 38–45.

Hopkins, P., & Pain, R. (2007). Geographies of age: Thinking relationally. *Area, 39*(3), 287–294.

Horton, R. (2020). It is not too early to learn lessons of a mismanaged response. *New Statesman*, 3–9 July, p. 48.

Hunter, A., & Suttles, G. (1972). The expanding community of limited liability. In G. Suttles (Ed.), *The social construction of communities*. Chicago, IL: Chicago University Press.

Hwang, J., Wang, L., Siever, J., Del Medico, T., & Jones, C. A. (2019). Loneliness and social isolation among older adults in a community exercise program: A qualitative study. *Aging & Mental Health*, 23(6), 736–742.

Jacobs, J. (1992). *The death and life of great American cities*. New York, NY: Vintage Books.

Jeffres, L. W., Bracken, C. C., Jian, G., & Casey, M. F. (2009). The impact of third places of community quality of life. *Applied Research Quality Life*, 4, 333–345.

Jenkin, C. R., Eime, R. M., Westerbeek, H., O'Sullivan, G., & van Uffelen, J. G. Z. (2016). Are they 'worth their weight in gold'? Sport for older adults: Benefits and barriers of their participation for sporting organisations. *International Journal of Sport Policy and Politics*, 8(4), 663–680.

Jennings, P. (2007). *The local: A history of the English pub*. Stroud: The History Press.

Jennings, V., & Bamkole, O. (2019). The relationship between social cohesion and urban green space: An avenue for health promotion. *International Journal of Environmental Research and Public Health*, 16, 452. 1–14.

Jones, G., Meegan, R., Kennett, P., & Croft, J. (2016). The uneven impact of austerity on the voluntary and community sector: A tale of two cities. *Urban Studies*, 53(10), 2064–2080.

Jones, H., Neal, S., Mohan, G., Connell, K., Cochrane, A., & Bennett, K. (2015). Urban multiculture and everyday encounter in semi-public, franchised café spaces. *The Sociological Review*, 63, 644–661.

Jopling, K., & Jones, D. (2018). *Age-friendly and inclusive volunteering: Review of community contributions in later life*. London: Centre for Ageing Better.

Joseph, D., & Southcott, J. (2019). Meaning of leisure for older people: An Australian study of line dancing. *Leisure Studies*, 38(1), 74–87.

Jupp, E. (2013). 'I feel more at home here than in my own community': Approaching the emotional geographies of neighbourhood policy'. *Critical Social Policy*, 33(3), 532–553.

Kaczynski, A. T., & Henderson, K. A. (2007). Environmental correlates of physical activity: A review of evidence about parks and recreation. *Leisure Sciences*, *29*(4), 315–354.

Kamalpour, M., Watson, J., & Buys, L. (2020). How can online communities support resilience factors among older adults. *International Journal of Human-Computer Interaction*, *36*(14), 1342–1353.

Kazmierczak, A. (2013). The contribution of local parks to neighbourhood social ties. *Landscape and Urban Planning*, *109*(1), 31–44.

Kelley, J. A., Dannerfer, D., & Masarwech, L. A. I. (2018). Addressing erasure, microfication and social change: Age-friendly initiatives and environmental gerontology in the 21st century. In T. Buffel, S. Handler, & C. Phillipson (Eds.), *Age-friendly cities and communities: A global perspective first edition*. Bristol: Policy Press.

Kelsey, T., & Kenny, M. (2021). *Townscapes: The value of social infrastructure. Policy report series*. Cambridge: Bennett Institute for Public Policy. Retrieved from https://www.bennettinstitute.cam.ac.uk/publications/social-infrastructure/

Kleiber, D., & Nimrod, G. (2009). 'I can't be very sad': Constraints and adaptations in the leisure of a learning in retirement group. *Leisure Studies*, *28*(1), 76–83.

Klinenberg, E. (2013). *Going solo: The extraordinary rise and surprising appeal of living alone*. London: Gerald Duckworth & Co. Ltd.

Klinenberg, E. (2015). *Heat wave: A social autopsy of disaster in chicago* (2nd ed.). Chicago, IL: University of Chicago Press.

Klinenberg, E. (2018). *Palaces for the people: How to build a more equal and united society*. London: The Bodley Head.

Lager, D., Van Hoven, D., & Huigen, P. P. (2013). Dealing with change in old age: Negotiating working-class belonging in the process or urban renewal in The Netherlands. *Geoforum*, *50*, 54–61.

Langston, T. (2011). It is life support, isn't it? Social capital in a community choir. *International Journal of Community Music*, *4*(2), 163–184.

Latham, A., & Layton, J. (2019). Social infrastructure and the public life of cities: Studying urban sociality and public spaces. *Geography Compass*, *13*(7), ee12444.

Laurier, E., & Philo, C. (2006). Cold shoulders and napkins handed: Gestures of responsibility. *Transactions of the Institute of British Geographers NS, 31,* 193–207.

Lewis, C., & Cotterell, N. (2017). *Social isolation and older black, Asian and minority ethnic people in Greater Manchester.* A report for ambition for ageing.

Lewis, C., Hammond, M., Kavanagh, N., Phillipson, C., & Yarker, S. (2020). *Developing age-friendly communities in the Northern Gateway urban regeneration project.* The University of Manchester. Retrieved from https://documents.manchester.ac.uk/display.aspx?DocID=46848

Ley, D. (2008). The immigrant church as an urban service hub. *Urban Studies, 45*(10), 2057–2074.

Linley, R. (2011). *Public libraries, older people and social exclusion.* Working Paper. Leeds: Leeds Metropolitan University.

Linnon, L. A., D'Angelo, H., Cherise, M. H. S., & Harrington, C. B. (2014). A literature synthesis of health promotion research in salons and barbershops. *American Journal of Preventative Medicine, 47*(1), 77–85.

Loane, S. S. (2015). *The co-creation of consumer value within online health communities.* Macquarie Park, NSW: Macquarie University, Faculty of Business and Economics, Department of Marketing and Management.

Lofland, L. H. (1998). *The public realm: Exploring the city's quintessential social territory.* New York, NY: Aldine de Gruyter.

Lucas, K., Stokes, G., Bastiaanssen, J., & Burkinshaw, J. (2019). Inequalities in mobility and access in the UK transport system. Future of Mobility: Evidence Review. Foresight, Government Office for Science. Retrieved from https://assets.publishing.service.gov.uk/government/uploads/system/uploads/attachment_data/file/784685/future_of_mobility_access.pdf

Lui, C. W., Everingham, J. A., Warburton, J., Cuthill, M., & Bartlett, H. (2009). What makes a community age-friendly: A review of international literature. *Australasian Journal on Ageing, 28*(3), 116–121.

Maas, J., Dillen van, M. E., Verheij, R. A., & Groenewegen, P. P. (2009). Social contacts as a possible mechanism behind the relation between green space and health. *Health & Place, 15,* 586–595.

MacCallum, J., & Palmer, D. (2006). *Community building through intergenerational exchange programs: Report to the National Youth Affairs*

Research Scheme (NYARS). Australian Government Department of Family and Community Services. Retrieved from https://core.ac.uk/reader/11233459

MacCallum, J., Palmer, D., Wright, P., Cumming-Potvin, W., Brooker, M., & Tero, C. (2010). Australian perspectives: Community building through intergenerational exchange programs. *Journal of Intergenerational Relationships, 8*(2), 113–127.

Macintyre, V. G., Cotterill, S., Anderson, J., Phillipson, C., Benton, J. S., & French, D. P. (2019). I would never come here because I've got my own garden: Perceptions of small urban green spaces. *International Journal of Environmental Research and Public Health, 16*(1994), 1–18.

Macmillan, R. (2011). Supporting the voluntary sector in an age of austerity: The UK coalition government's consultation on improving support for frontline civil society organisations in England. *Voluntary Sector Review, 2*(1), 115–124.

Maidment, J., & Macfarlane, S. (2009). Craft groups: Sites of friendship, empowerment, belonging and learning for older women. *Groupwork, 19*(1), 10–25.

Mainey, A. (2019). *What have we learned about street outreach with older people?* Operational strategies from the Ageing Better in Camden Outreach Team. Age UK Camden.

Markman, A. (2012). It is motivating to belong to a group. *Psychology Today.*

Marmot, M., Allen, J., Boyce, T., Goldblatt, P., & Morrison, J. (2020a). *Health equity in England: The marmot review 10 years on.* London: UCL Institute of Health Equity.

Marmot, M., Allen, J., Goldblatt, P., Herd, E., & Morrison, J. (2020b). Build back fairer: The COVID-19 marmot review. In *The pandemic, socioeconomic and health inequalities in England.* London: Institute of Health Equity.

McClain, J., Gullatt, K., & Lee, C. (2018). *Resilience and protective factors in older adults.* Graduate Master's Theses, Capstones, and Culminating Projects. 296. doi:10.33015/dominican.edu/2018.OT.11

Mele, C., Ng, M., & Bo Chim, M. (2015). Urban markets as a 'corrective' to advanced urbanism: The social space of wet markets in contemporary Singapore. *Urban Studies, 52*(1), 103–120.

Melville, J., & Bernard, J. (2011). Intergenerational shared sites: Policy and practice developments in the UK. *Journal of Intergenerational Relationships*, 9(3), 237–249.

Miller, E. (2016). Beyond bingo. *Journal of Leisure Research*, 48(1), 35–49.

Milligan, C., Gatrell, A., & Bingley, A. (2004). 'Cultivating health': Therapeutic landscapes and older people in Northern England. *Social Science & Medicine*, 58, 1781–1793.

Milligan, C., Neary, D., Payne, S., Hanratty, B., Irwin, P., & Dowrick, C. (2016). Older men and social activity: A scoping review of men's sheds and other gendered interventions. *Ageing and Society*, 36, 895–923.

Minton, A. (2006). *Ground control: Fear and happiness in the twenty-first-century city*. London: Penguin.

Morales, A. (2009). Public markets as community development tools. *Journal of Planning Education and Research*, 28, 426–440.

Morse, N., & Munro, E. (2018). 'Museums' community engagement schemes, austerity and practices of care in two local museum services. *Social and Cultural Geography*, 19(3), 357–378.

Muddiman, D., Durrani, S., Pateman, J., Dutch, M., Linley, R., & Vincent, J. (2001). *Open to all? The public library and social exclusion*. London: Council for Museums, Archives and Libraries.

Musselwhite, C. (2017). Exploring the importance of discretionary mobility in later life. *Working with Older People*, 21(1), 49–58.

Musselwhite, C., & Haddad, H. (2010). Mobility, accessibility and quality of later life. *Quality in Ageing and Older Adults*, 11(1), 25–37.

Musselwhite, C., & Haddad, H. (2018). Older people's travel and mobility needs: A reflection of a hierarchical model 10 years on. *Quality in Ageing and Older Adults*, 19(2), 87–105.

Naughton, L. (2014). Geographical narratives of social capital: Telling different stories about the socio-economy with context, space, place, power and agency. *Progress in Human Geography*, 38(1), 3–21.

Neal, S., Bennett, K., Jones, H., Cochrane, A., & Mohan, G. (2015). Multicultural and public parks: Researching super-diversity and attachment in pubic green space. *Population, Space and Place*, 21, 436–475.

Nichols, G., Findlay-King, L., & Forbes, D. (2020). The community asset transfer of leisure facilities in the UK: A review and research agenda. *Voluntas, 31*, 1159–1172.

Noble, G. (2011). Belonging in Bennelong: Ironic inclusion and cosmopolitan joy in John Howard's (former) electorate. In K. Jacobs & J. Malpas (Eds.), *Ocean to outback: Cosmopolitanism in contemporary Australia* (pp. 150–174). Crawley: UWA Press.

Ofcom. (2017). Rise of the social seniors revealed. Retrieved from https://www.ofcom.org.uk/about-ofcom/latest/media/media-releases/2017/rise-social-seniors

Office of National Statistics (ONS). (2019). *Internet users*, UK: 2019. Retrieved from https://www.ons.gov.uk/businessindustryandtrade/itandinternetindustry/bulletins/internetusers/2019

Oldenburg, R. (1989). *The great good places*. New York, NY: Paragon House.

Oldenburg, R., & Bissett, D. (1982). The third place. *Qualitative Sociology, 5*, 265–284.

Onward. (2020). Covid-19 and community. Retrieved from https://www.ukonward.com/covid-19-and-community/

Orellana, K., Manthorpe, J., & Tinker, A. (2020a). Day centres for older people: A systematically conducted scoping review of literature about their benefits, purposes and how they are perceived. *Ageing & Society, 40*, 73–104.

Orellana, K., Manthorpe, J., & Tinker, A. (2020b). Day centres for older people-attender characteristics, access routes and outcomes of regular attendance: Findings of exploratory mixed methods case study research. *BMC Geriatrics, 20*, 158.

Overmans, T., & Timms-Arnold, K.-T. (2016). Managing austerity: Comparing municipal austerity plans in The Netherlands and North Rhine-Westphaila. *Public Management Review, 18*(7), 1043–1062.

OXFAM. (2012). *The perfect storm: Economic stagnation, the rising cost of living, public spending cuts, and the impact of UK poverty*. London: Oxfam.

Pahl, R., & Spencer, L. (2004). Personal communities: Not simply families of fate or choice. *Current Sociology, 52*(2), 199–221.

Pain, R. (2001). Gender, race, age and fear in the city. *Urban Studies, 38*(5–6), 899–913.

Pain, R. (2005). Intergenerational relations and practice in the development of sustainable communities. Background paper for the Office of Deputy Prime Minister: International Centre for Regeneration and Regional and Development Studies (ICRRDS), Durham University.

Pain, R. (2019). Chronic urban trauma: The slow violence of housing dispossession. *Urban Studies*, *56*(2), 285–400.

Parkhurst, G., Galvin, K., Musselwhite, C., Phillips, J., Shergold, I., & Todres, L. (2014). Beyond transport: Understanding the role of mobilities in connecting rural elders in civic society. In C. Hennesey, R. Means, & V. Burholt (Eds.), *Countryside connections: Older people, community, and place in rural Britain* (pp. 125–175). Bristol: Policy Press.

Pateman, J. (1999). Public libraries, social exclusion and social class. *Information for Social Change*, *10*, 3–12.

Peck, J. (2012). Austerity urbanism. *City*, *16*(6), 626–655.

Penny, J. (2020). 'Defend the Ten': Everyday dissensus against the slow spoiling of Lambeth's libraries. *Environment and Planning D: Society and Space*, *38*(5), 923–940.

Peters, K., Elands, B., & Buijs, A. (2010). Social interactions in urban parks: Stimulating social cohesion? *Urban Forestry & Urban Greening*, *9*, 93–100.

Petric, G. (2014). Perceived quality of conversations in online communities: Conceptual framework, scale development, and empirical validation. *Cyberpsychology, Behaviour and Social Networking*, *17*(2), 82–90.

Phillipson, C. (2015). Placing ethnicity at the centre of studies of later life: Theoretical perspectives and empirical challenges. *Ageing & Society*, *35*(5), 917–934.

Phillipson, C., Bernard, M., Phillips, J., & Orr, J. (2001). *The family and community life of older people*. London: Routledge.

Phillipson, C., Lang, L., Yarker, S., Lewis, C., Doran, P., Goff, M., & Buffel, T. (2021). *COVID-19 and social exclusion: Experiences of older people living in areas of multiple deprivation*. Manchester Institute for Collaborative Research on Ageing. Retrieved from https://documents.manchester.ac.uk/display.aspx?DocID=56003

Portas, M. (2011). The portas review: An independent review into the future of our high streets. Retrieved from https://assets.publishing.service.gov.uk/government/uploads/system/uploads/attachment_data/file/6292/2081646.pdf

Power, A., & Hall, E. (2018). Placing care in times of austerity. *Social and Cultural Geography*, *19*(3), 303–313.

Putnam, R. (1993a). *Making democracy work: Civic traditions in modern Italy*. Princeton, NJ: Princeton University Press.

Putnam, R. (1993b). The prosperous community: Social capital and public life. *The American Prospect*, *13*, 35–42.

Putnam, R. (2000). *Bowling alone: The collapse and revival of American community*. New York, NY: Simon and Schuster.

Ranganathan, S. R. (1931). *The five laws of library science*. Madras: The Madras Library Association.

Raynes, N. V., & Rawlings, B. (2004). Recreating social capital. *Journal of Intergenerational Relationships*, *2*(1), 6–28.

Ritzer, G. (2006). *McDonalidzation: The reader*. Thousand Oaks, CA: Pine Forge Press.

Ritzer, G. (2008). *The McDonalization of society* (5th ed.). Thousand Oaks, CA: Pine Forge Press.

Rivlin, P., & González, S. (2018). Public markets: Spaces for sociability under threat? The case of Leeds' Kirkgate Market. In S. González (Ed.), *Contested markets contested cities: Gentrification and urban justice in retail spaces* (pp. 131–149). London: Routledge.

Robinson, K. (2020). Everyday multiculturalism in the public library: Taking knitting together seriously. *Sociology*, *54*(3), 556–572.

Robinson, K., & Sheldon, R. (2019). Witnessing loss in the everyday: Community buildings in austerity Britain. *The Sociological Review*, *67*(1), 111–125.

Rosenbaum, M. S. (2006). Exploring the social supportive role of third place in consumers' lives. *Journal of Service Research*, *9*(1), 59–72.

Rosenbaum, M. S., Ward, J., Walker, B. A., & Ostrom, A. L. (2007). A cup of coffee with a dash of love: An investigation of commercial social support and third-place attachment. *Journal of Service Research*, *10*(1), 43–59.

Rowles, G. D. (1983). Place and personal identity in old age: Observations from Appalachia. *Journal of Environmental Psychology*, *3*(4), 299–313.

Rúa, M. M. (2017). Ageing in displacement: Urban revitalisation and Puerto Rican elderhood in Chicago. *Anthropology & Ageing*, *38*(1), 44–59.

Scharf, T. (2011). 'Loneliness: An urban perspective' Safeguarding the convoy: A call to action from the Campaign to End Loneliness. London: Age UK.

Scharf, T., & De Jong Gierveld, J. (2008). Loneliness in urban neighbourhoods: And Anglo-Dutch comparison. European Journal of Ageing, 5(2), 103–115.

Scharlach, A. E. (2016). Age-friendly cities: For whom? By whom? For what purpose? In T. Moulaert & S. Garon (Eds.), Age-friendly cities and communities in international Comparison (pp. 305–331). New York, NY: Springer International Publishing.

Schofield-Tomschin, S., & Littrell, M. (2001). Textile handcraft guild participation: A conduit to successful aging. Clothing and Textiles Research Journal, 19(2), 41–51.

Schuller, T. (2007). Reflections on the use of social capital. Review of Social Economy, 65(1), 11–28.

Sennett, R. (1974). The fall of public man. New York, NY: Norton.

Sennett, R. (2017). Building and dwelling: Ethnics for the city. London: Penguin.

Shaw, I. G. (2019). Worlding austerity: The spatial violence of poverty. Society and Space: D, 37(6), 971–989.

Sherbourne, C. D., & Stewart, A. L. (1991). The MOS social support survey. Social Science and Medicine, 32(6), 705–714.

Shinew, K. J., Glover, T. D., & Parry, D. C. (2004). Leisure spaces as potential sites for interracial interaction: Community gardens in urban areas. Journal of Leisure Research, 36, 336–355.

Simmel, G. (1949). The sociology of sociability. American Journal of Sociology, 55(3), 254–261. (translated by E. Hughes).

Skeggs, B. (2014). Values beyond value? Is anything beyond the logic of capital? British Journal of Sociology, 65, 1–20.

Smith, A. (2021). Sustaining municipal parks in an era of neoliberal austerity: The contested commercialisation of Gunnersbury Park. Environment and Planning A: Economy and Space, 53(4), 704–722.

Smith, R. J., Lehning, A. J., & Kim, K. (2018). Ageing in place in a gentrifying neighbourhoods: Implications for physical and mental health. The Geronotologist, 58(1), 26–35.

Solnit, R. (2009). *A paradise built in hell*. New York, NY: Penguin.

Stack, C. (1996). *Call to home: African Americans reclaim the rural south*. New York, NY: Basic Books.

Stanton, G. (2003). Intergenerational storytelling bringing the generations together in North Tyneside. *Journal of Intergenerational Relationships, 1*(1), 71–80.

Stebbins, R. A. (1982). Serious leisure: A conceptual statement. *Pacific Sociological Review, 25*, 251–272.

Stewart, J., Browning, C., & Sims, J. (2015). Civic socialising: A revealing new theory about older people's social relationships. *Ageing & Society, 35*, 750–764.

Stone, G. P. (1954). City shoppers and urban identification: Observations on the social psychology of city life. *American Journal of Sociology, 60*(July), 36–45.

Tanner, W., O'Shaughnessy, J., Krasniqi, F., & Blagden, J. (2020). The state of our social fabric: Measuring the changing nature of community over time and geography. Onward Report. Retrieved from https://www.ukonward.com/socialfabric/

Thang, L. L. (2001). *Generations in touch: Linking the old and young in a Tokyo neighbourhood*. Ithaca, NY: Cornell University Press.

The Guardian. (2019). Retrieved from https://www.theguardian.com/business/2019/jul/22/banks-accused-abandoning-england-poorest-communities

Thrift, N. (2005). But malice afterthought: Cities and the natural history of hatred. *Transactions of the Institute of British Geographers, NS 30*, 133–150.

Thurnell-Read, T. (2020). 'If they weren't in the pub, they probably wouldn't even know each other': Alcohol, sociability and pub based leisure. *International Journal of the Sociology of Leisure, 4*, 61–78.

Toepoel, V. (2013). Ageing, leisure, and social connectedness: How could leisure help reduce social isolation of older people. *Social Indices Research, 113*, 355–372.

Tomaney, J., & Pike, A. (2020). Levelling up? *The Political Quarterly, 91*(1), 43–48.

Valentine, G. (2008). Living with difference: Reflections on geographies of encounter. *Progress in Human Geography, 32*(3), 323–337.

Van den Berg, A. E., Van Winsum-Westra, M., de Vries, S., & van Dillen, S. (2010). Allotment gardening and health: A comparative survey among allotment gardens and their neighbours without an allotment. *Environmental Health*, *9*, 74.

Vanderbeck, R. M. (2007). Intergenerational geographies: Age relations, segregation and re-engagements. *Geography Compass*, *1/2*, 200–221.

Vanderbeck, R., & Worth, N. (2014). *Intergenerational space*. London: Routledge.

Vårheim, A. (2009). Public libraries: Places creating social capital? *Library Hi Tech*, *27*(3), 372–381.

Veitch, J., Flowers, E., Ball, K., Deforche, B., & Timperio, A. (2020). Designing parks for older adults: A qualitative study using walk-along interviews. *Urban Forestry & Urban Greening*, *54*, 126768.

Versey, H. S. (2018). A tale of two Harlems: Gentrification, social capital and implications for ageing in place. *Social Science & Medicine*, *214*, 1–11.

Victor, C., Burholt, V., & Martin, W. (2012). Loneliness and minority ethnic elders in Great Britain: An exploratory study. *Journal of Cross-Cultural Gerontology*, *27*, 65–78.

Victor, C. R., & Pikhartova, J. (2020). Lonely places or lonely people? Investigating the relationship between loneliness and place of residence. *BMC Public Health*, *20*, 778.

Ward Thompson, C. (2013). Activity, exercise and the planning and design of outdoor spaces. *Journal of Environmental Psychology*, *34*, 79–96.

Ward, R., Clark, A., Campbell, S., Graham, B., Kullberg, A., Manji, K., ... Keady, J. (2018). The lived neighbourhood: Understanding how people with dementia engage with their local environment. *Intergenerational Psychogeriatrics*, *30*(6), 867–880.

Warr, P. (1987). *Work, unemployment and mental health*. Oxford: Clarendon Press.

Watson, S., & Studdert, D. (2006). *Markets as sites for social interaction: Spaces of diversity*. A report for Joseph Rowntree Foundation. London: Policy Press.

Wilson, H. F. (2017). On geography and encounter: Bodies, borders, and difference. *Progress in Human Geography*, *41*(4), 451–471.

Wiltshire, G., & Stevinson, C. (2018). Exploring the role of social capital in community-based physical activity: Qualitative insights form *parkrun*. *Qualitative Research in Sport, Exercise and Health, 10*(1), 47–62.

Wink, P., & Dillon, M. (2003). Religiousness, spirituality, and psychosocial functioning in late adulthood: Findings from a longitudinal study. *Psychology and Aging, 18*(4), 916–924.

Wise, A. (2005). Hope and belonging in a multicultural suburb. *Journal of Intercultural Studies, 26*(1–2), 171–186.

Wolch, J. R. (1989). The shadow state: Transformations in the voluntary sector. In J. D. Wolch & M. Dear (Eds.), *The power of geography: How territory shapes social life* (pp. 197–221). London: Unwin Hyman.

Worpole, K., & Knox, K. (2007). *The social value of public places.* The Joseph Rowntree Foundation. Retrieved from https://www.jrf.org.uk/sites/default/files/jrf/migrated/files/2050-public-space-community.pdf

Yarker, S. (2018). Tangential attachments: Towards a more nuanced understanding of the impacts of cultural urban regeneration on local identities. *Urban Studies, 55*(15), 3421–3436.

Yarker, S. (2019). Reconceptualising comfort as part of local belonging: The use of confidence, commitment and irony. *Social and Cultural Geography, 20*(4), 534–550.

Yarker, S. (2020). Ageing in place for minority ethnic communities: The importance of social infrastructure. A report for Ambition for Ageing.

Yarker, S. (2021). A research agenda for geographies of intergenerational encounter. *Area, 53*(2), 264–271.

Yuen, F., & Johnson, A. J. (2017). Leisure spaces, community, and third places. *Leisure Sciences, 39*(3), 295–303.

INDEX